LIBRARY AND INFORMATION SCIENCE IN CHANGING PARADIGM

Library and Information Science in Changing Paradigm

Sambhu Nath Halder
Sibsankar Jana

Ess Ess Publications
New Delhi

Library and Information Science in Changing Paradigm

ISBN: 978-81-7000-696-1

₹ 825/-

First Published 2013

Published by:
Ess Ess Publications
4831/24, Ansari Road,
Darya Ganj,
New Delhi-110 002.
INDIA
Phones: 23260807, 41563444
Fax: 41563334
E-mail: info@essessreference.com
www.essessreference.com

Cover Design by *Patch Creative Unit*

Printed and bound in India at Salasar Imaging Systems.

Dedicated to
our loving parents
SHRI SUNIL KUMAR HALDER & SMT. CHANDANA HALDER
and
SHRI EKADASHI JANA & SMT. PARUL JANA

Contents

Preface

The book *Library and Information Science in Changing Paradigm* is an attempt to throw light on the role of library professionals and related topics in the contemporary society. The information and knowledge play the most important role in the present knowledge society and these are the central force and strategic resource of the society. A large number of information both in traditional and digital nature are coming out in every moment. These huge numbers of information is required to be organized, preserved and disseminated. Therefore we need to enrich and equip library and information profession to cope with the digital information overload situation.

At first we have discussed the genesis and origin of libraries in different parts of the world, different types of libraries from different viewpoints. Later we have enumerated the various highways and byways of LIS education in India.

Innovation of Information and Communication Technologies and different software's application in the field of Library and Information Science (LIS) create changes in entire library management system. This book highlights the present scenarios of LIS profession and the professional role in this changing environment. The new roles of LIS professionals especially as advocate, consortia manager, consultant, content manager, facilitator, guide or teacher, intermediary, knowledge manager, researcher, sifter, detector and instructor of plagiarism, information filter, intelligent agents, end-users' trainer/ educator, web site builder or publisher, interface designer, biblio-therapist / information therapist and change agents for institutional repositories, etc. are discussed. Side by side we talked about roles of government bodies, professional organizations and LIS schools to upgrade the managerial skills of LIS professionals to be fit for the changing situation.

In the electronic information environment the e-literacy is more or less same as literacy. It is recognized that computer literacy + information literacy (+ moral or ethical literacy) = e-literacy. We all must have the preliminary knowledge about the nature and use of electronic information.

Nowadays, LIS professionals are facing some international issues like cyberspace, content regulation, copyright, sense of community, digital preservation, marketing of information product and services, open source software, etc. are also discussed briefly. The book covers the prospects and opportunities to cope with the changes in library world from traditional to digital environment and towards knowledgebased society.

We hope that the library planners, professionals, students, teachers and researchers of Library and Information Science may be benefited from this book.

Sambhu Nath Halder

Sibsankar Jana

Foreword

Everywhere in both professional and popular literature we are reading about changing paradigm or paradigm shift. Paradigm first appeared in English in the 15th century, meaning "an example or pattern," and it still bears this meaning today. Since the 1960s, paradigm has been used in science to refer to thought pattern or a theoretical framework in any scientific discipline or other epistemological context. Historian of science Thomas Kuhn, in his book *The Structure of Scientific Revolutions (1970),* gave the word paradigm its contemporary meaning when he adopted it to refer to the set of practices that define a scientific discipline during a particular period of time. Dr. Dahalberg first introduced Kuhn's theory on paradigm in knowledge organization. She pointed out the existence of paradigms in the knowledge organization field and took the paradigm shift into our field by Ranganathan as an example. Librarianship, as a profession, emanated through accumulation of ideas from various professionals entities. Such accumulation of ideas has to face a new theoretical situation, leading to value added new paradigms at different points of time. This situation, in turn, calls for the acquisition of new range of skills on the part of the library and information service professionals which can apply to the wide range of contexts of various library and information activities.

In view of the emerging network environment (i.e. '*any time any place information*' paradigm of the networked environment), in view of the fundamental shift in goals of the library, and in view of the changes in information storage and delivery mechanisms, the domain of Library and Information Science (LIS) should cater to the needs of these changed setting by including the knowledge and skills required to function effectively in such an environment. Information resources are considered as intellectual capital in the global context. LIS professionals needs to accomplish their aim of the development, deployment, and management of information resources and services both in print and electronic media. They are to be prepared for information-based solutions in all contexts of the society, and to provide the competitive edge for the knowledge-based organization. The contemporary LIS professionals are required to live successfully in two time zones – the present and future; and this can only be achieved through the continuous improvement of the right skills and knowledge.

Under the said objective conditions, it is very pleasure to see that Sri Sambhu Nath Halder and Sri Shibsankar Jana have demonstrated a deep understanding of the major emerging areas of the LIS in their book entitled *Library and Information Science in Changing Paradigm*, which are very much relevant to the wide range of contexts with which library professionals are concerned and on which their professional practices are to be based. This book presents a systematic approach to the challenges of changing paradigm of library and information science, and puts issues like the journey of libraries from the period of bricks to byte, LIS education, new knowledge skills required in changing environment, e-literacy and the role of LIS professionals into appropriate context of modern perspective. It provides students and practitioners with a broad understanding of the major facets of LIS. Each chapter of this book deserves a book's length of justification. I fervently believe that this book is a commendable publication and distinct contribution to the discipline of Library and Information Science.

Dr. Juran Krishna Sarkhel
Professor,
Department of Library & Information Science
University of Kalyani
Kalyani—741235, West Bengal

Acknowledgements

The authors would like to record a great debt of gratitude to the following people for their technical and psychological support in the production of this book.

Dr. (Ms) Deepali Singhee and *Mr. Yudhisthir Halder,* for believing in us and their continuous inspiration for a book publication.

Ms. Radha Ravindran and *Ms. Mitali Mazumdar,* who did the proof-reading of the manuscript many times; they have performed a valuable service because writers often see what they intended to write, and thus fail to detect errors.

Prof. Juran Krishna Sarkhel, Prof. Sabuj Dasgupta, Prof. Dibyendu Paul, Prof. Goutam Maity and Mr. Arup Raychaudhury, for their blessing hand laying on our heads since LIS schooling time and their valuable suggestions in day to day chores.

We would not miss the opportunity to remember the names of some eminent Teachers and LIS Professionals for their contribution to this field and well wishes to us: *Prof. Amit Kumar Bandyopadhyay, Prof. Amitabha Chatterjee, Prof. Arjun Dasgupta, Dr. Arun Kumar Chakraborty, Dr. Asitabha Das, Dr. B.K. Sen, Dr. Bablu Sutradhar, Prof. Bhubaneswar Chakraborty, Dr. Binod Bihari Das, Prof. Biplab Chakraborty, Prof. Chaitali Dutta, Prof. Durga Sankar Rath, Dr. J.N. Satpathi, Prof. Krishnapada Majumder, Mr. Manilal Murmu, Mr. Mriganka Mandal, Mr. Narayan Ghosh, Prof. Partha Sarathi Mukherjee, Prof Pijushkanti Jana, Prof Pijushkanti Panigrahi, Prof. Pinaki Nath Mukhopadhyay, Prof. Ramkrishna Saha, Prof. Ratna Bandyopadhyay,*

Prof. Salil Ch. Khan, Dr. Soumitra Sarkar, Prof. Subalchandra Biswas, Prof. Subarna Kumar Das, Prof. Sunil Kr. Chatterjee, Prof. Tarun K. Mondal, Dr. V.K. Thomas, Prof Udayan Bhattacharya.

Last but not the least; we would like to thank all stakeholders of Ess Ess Publications for their effort to publish this book at the earliest.

Sambhu Nath Halder
Sibsankar Jana

1

Library in Changing Paradigm

1.1 DEFINITION OF LIBRARY

Library is a temple of learning. The word "Library" is derived from the Latin word "liber" which means- a Book. Earlier a library was "a place where books were written". The term 'Library' was frequently used as a "collection of books" and a librarian as a keeper or guard of books. This word 'Library' has taken centuries to become central point of all social actions and has got recognition as a social institution. A library is an organized collection of resources made accessible to a defined community for reference or borrowing. It provides physical or digital access to material, and may be confined in a physical building or room, or a virtual space, or both. Collections can include books, periodicals, newspapers, manuscripts, films, maps, prints, documents, microform, CDs, cassettes, videotapes, DVDs, video games, e-books, audio-books and other formats. Libraries range in size from a few shelves of books to several million items (Wikipedia, Library, 2012). Library is a social organisation. It has been created as an integral part of communication, as required by society and culture.

Library ensures continuity of a culture and connects culture of different ages.

1.2 HISTORY

1.2.1. Early History

The library has a long history. Before going through the libraries' origin, it is necessary to know the nature of writing materials or documents in the ancient libraries. The in-scribed clay tablets of near about 3000 B.C. have been discovered among the archaeological remains of the Sumerians of southern Mesopotamia. The banks of the Nile were covered with papyrus plants – from which the Egyptians made a form of paper in ancient times. However, Mesopotamia's rivers had its land did provide good clay, and consequently the clay tablet became the standard material. Unlike other writing materials such as paper, leather and wood, it is hard and more durable.

Therefore, when a conqueror set a Mesopotamian palace ablaze, he helped to ensure the survival of any clay tablets in it. These clay, moreover, is cheap, and fashioning it into tablets is easy, factors helped the clay tablet the preferred writing material not only throughout Mesopotamia but far outside it as well, in Syria, Asia Minor, Persia, and for a while in Crete and Greece. Excavators have unearthed clay tablets in all these lands. In the land in certain areas, they lasted down to the beginning of the Christian era until finally yielding, for the last time, to more convenient alternatives (Casson, Lionel, 2001).

The Greece and Rome were the first to use some of the fundamental library procedures such as the identification of individual works through titling; the gathering of similar works into series; the creation of catalogues etc. In addition, they were the first to suffer from some of the fundamental library ills: theft and abuse of the holdings. In describing the building complex of "Ozy-mandias" by a Greek historian of the first century B.C., Diodorus - his name for Ramses II (1279–1213 B.C.) - Diodorus tells that it included a "sacred library" and even in the cites the inscription bore, "Clinic for the Soul." The libraries were very different as per limited scope and purpose in the Near East, from the library as we know it, with shelves full of books on all subjects and doors open to readers with interests in all subjects. Such a library had to await the coming of the Greeks. For they were a people endowed with what was needed to bring it into existence - a high level of literacy and an abiding interest in intellectual endeavor. It comes true, when the Greeks first appear in history, during the Mycenaean Age in 1600 to 1200 B.C.; they were more like their contemporaries in the Near East. This is the age reflected in the epics of Homer, in whose narrative the land is ruled by all-powerful monarchs holding court in impressive palaces amid the trappings of great wealth, the likes of Agamemnon and Menelaus. For long the picture he presented was thought to be the stuff of mythology. Then, in the nineteenth century, archaeologists began to unearth remains that revealed the sober reality behind Homer's words—the ruins of massive city walls, of many-roomed palaces, of mighty tombs. They even found writings. The language was an early form of Greek but, as in the Near East, the writing was on clay tablets and in a syllabic form of script. Thousands have been excavated from the palaces of ruins. To the great disappointment of the discoverers, none were literary in content; without exception they were humdrum records presumably connected with palace administration (Casson, Lionel, 2001).

The library of Alexandria, founded in and around 300 B.C., was the first of its kind, and throughout ancient history remained the greatest of its kind. Yet it seems to have suddenly sprung into being. Its nearest match in size, Ashurbanipal's library, was for the king's use and specialized in materials for his particular needs. The collection Aristotle put together, despite its extent and variety, was strictly personal, a tool for his multifarious studies. The library of Alexandria was comprehensive, embracing books of all sorts from everywhere, and it was public, open to anyone with fit-ting scholarly or literary qualifications. The spectacular campaign of Alexander the Great that won for him an empire stretching from his homeland in Macedon to the western border of India transformed the Greek world. Until then most Greeks had been citizens of city-states—mini-nations consisting of a city and its immediate surroundings. More than 30,000 clay tablets from the *Library of Ashurbanipal* have come upon at Nineveh, providing modern scholars with an amazing wealth of Mesopotamian literary, religious and administrative work. Among the findings were the *Enuma Elish*, also known as *the Epic of Creation*, which depicts a traditional Babylonian view of creation, the *Epic of Gilgamesh*, a large selection of "omen texts" including *Enuma Anu Enlil* which "contained omens dealing with the moon, its visibility, eclipses, and conjunction with planets and fixed stars, the sun, its corona, spots, and eclipses, the weather, namely lightning, thunder, and clouds, and the planets and their visibility, appearance, and stations", and astronomic/astrological texts, as well as standard lists used by scribes and scholars such as word lists, bilingual vocabularies, lists of signs and synonyms, and lists of medical diagnoses. The celebrated book collectors of Hellenistic Antiquity were listed in the late 2nd century in *Deipnosophistae.* The cultivated Hellenized diners in *Deipnosophistae* pass over the libraries of Rome in silence. By the time of Augustus there were public libraries near the forums of Rome: there were libraries in the *Porticus Octaviae* near the *Theatre of Marcellus*, in the temple of Apollo Palatinus, and in the Bibliotheca Ulpiana in the *Forum of Trajan*. Private or personal libraries made up of non-fiction and fiction books appeared in classical Greece in the 5th century BC. The state archives were kept in a structure on the slope between the *Roman Forum* and the *Capitoline Hill* (e-note, 2012). In the West, the first public libraries were established under the *Roman Empire* as each succeeding emperor strove to open one or many which outshone that of his predecessor. Unlike the Greek libraries, readers had direct access to the scrolls, which were kept on shelves built into the walls of a large room. Reading or copying was normally done in the room itself. The surviving records give only a few instances of lending features. As a rule, Roman public libraries were bilingual: they had a Latin room and a Greek room. Most of the large *Roman baths* were also cultural centers, built from the start with a library, a two room arrangement with one room for Greek and one for Latin texts (Wikipedia, Library, 2012).

Libraries were filled with parchment scrolls as at *Library of Pergamum* and on papyrus scrolls as at Alexandria: the export of prepared writing materials was a staple of commerce. There were a few institutional or royal libraries which were open to an educated public (such as the Serapeum collection of the *Library of Alexandria*, once the largest library in the ancient world), but overall collections were private. In those rare cases where it was possible for a scholar to consult library books there seems to have been no direct access to the stacks. In all recorded cases, the books were kept in a relatively small room where the staff went to get them for the readers, who had to consult them in an adjoining hall or covered walkway.

In the 6th century, at the very close of the *Classical period*, the great libraries of the Mediterranean world remained those of Constantinople and Alexandria. *Cassiodorus*, minister to Theodoric, established a monastery at Vivarium in the heel of Italy with a library to bring Greek learning to Latin readers and preserve texts both sacred and secular for future generations. As its unofficial librarian, Cassiodorus not only collected as many manuscripts as he could, he also wrote treatises aimed at instructing his monks in the proper uses of reading and methods for copying texts accurately. In the end, however, the library at Vivarium was dispersed and lost within a century (Wikipedia, Scriptorium, 2012). Old texts were washed off and the valuable parchment and papyrus were reused, forming palimpsests. As scrolls gave way to the new book-form, the codex was universally used for Christian literature.

Tian Yi Ge is an ancient library and garden in China. It is one of the top tourist attractions at Ningbo in China. The imperial library is the oldest library in China. As per the record, Han Chinese scholar Liu Hsiang established the first library classification system during the Han Dynasty and also the first book notation system. Then the library catalog was generally written on scrolls of fine silk and stored in silk bags. Buddhist scriptures, educational materials and histories were stored in libraries in pre-modern Southeast Asia. King *Anawrahta* founded a royal library in Myanmar named the *Pitaka Taik*. British envoy Michael Symes, upon visiting this library in the 18th century described that "it is not improbable that his Birman majesty may possess a more numerous library than any potentate, from the banks of the Danube to the borders of China". In Thailand, libraries named *ho trai* were built throughout the country, usually on stilts above a pond to prevent bugs from eating at the books (Wikipedia, Library, 2012).

1.2.2. Early Modern Libraries

Started from the 15th century in Italy, the assembled libraries with care and persistence of humanists and their patrons provided a nucleus around which an academy of scholars gathered in each Italian city of consequence. Cosimo de Medici in Florence established his own collection, which formed the basis of the *Laurentian Library*. In Rome, the papal collections were brought together by Pope Nicholas V, in separate Greek and Latin libraries, and housed by Pope Sixtus IV, who consigned the Bibliotheca Apostolica Vaticana to the care of his librarian, the humanist *Bartolomeo Platina* in February 1475. In the 16th century *Sixtus V* bisected Bramante's Cortile del Belvedere with a cross-wing to house the Apostolic Library in suitable magnificence. The 16th and 17th centuries saw other privately endowed libraries assembled in Rome: the Vallicelliana, formed from the books of Saint *Filippo Neri*, with other distinguished libraries such as that of *Cesare Baronio*, the Biblioteca Angelica founded by the Augustinian Angelo Rocca, which was the only truly public library in Counter-Reformation Rome; the Biblioteca Alessandrina with which Pope Alexander VII endowed the University of Rome; the Biblioteca Casanatense of the Cardinal *Girolamo Casanate*; and finally the Biblioteca Corsiniana founded by the bibliophile Clement XII Corsini and his nephew Cardinal Neri Corsini, still housed in Palazzo Corsini in via della Lungara.

The period between 1600 and 1700 was called the "golden age of libraries". In this period numbers of books had risen and cost had come down, nationalism was encouraging nations to build great libraries. Some of the more important libraries include the Bodleian Library at Oxford, the Library of the British Museum, the Mazarine

Library and the Bibliothèque Sainte-Geneviève in Paris, and the National Central Library in Italy, the Prussian State Library, the M.E. Saltykov-Shchedrin State Public Library of St. Petersburg, and many more. *Literature of Libraries in the Seventeenth and Eighteenth Centuries* was a collection of nine short works from the period which was published by John Cotton Dana and Henry W. Kent in 1906-07 (Wikipedia, Library, 2012).

1.2.3. Current Trends in Library

Change is the dominant factor of human life. There is immense importance to change in present period and it is the cause of human progress. According to Halder (2009) change is one reality with which individuals, groups and organizations must constantly cope in order to survive. The needs for progressive changes in people's attitudes and behaviors are essential for global acceptance. The Library and Information Science is no exception to this. Nevertheless for Library and Information Science (LIS) professionals, a change is often linked with modern information technologies and management issues (Bhaurao, 2010).

Over the past few decades, the nature of library environment and mode of service has changed drastically. With the development and application of Information and Communication Technologies (ICTs), the library environment has shifted as: the traditional library, hybrid library, automated library, digital library, virtual library, Library 2.0. With such changes, the structure and nature of library and side by side the LIS profession has also changed in a dynamic way. Now in this present situation the LIS professionals are playing all-round multimodal roles to satisfy the different approaches of the end users. Library is a vast storehouse of information. Emergence of Information and Communication Technology (ICT) libraries has been acquiring different approaches of the same and mode of service is changed. Therefore, different types of libraries have born in society (Halder, 2009).

1.3. TYPES OF LIBRARY

1.3.1. Libraries on the basis of nature of collection and services

1.3.1.1. Traditional Library

A traditional library (WTEC Hyper-Librarian, 1999) is characterized by the following:

- emphasis on storage and preservation of physical items, particularly books and periodicals.
- cataloging at a high level rather than one of detail, e.g., author and subject indexes as opposed to full text.
- browsing based on physical proximity of related materials, e.g., books on sociology are near one another on the shelves.
- passivity; information is physically assembled in one place; users must travel to the library to learn what is there and make use of it.

1.3.1.2. Hybrid Library

The hybrid library is a term used to describe libraries containing a mix of traditional print library resources and a growing number of electronic resources. Hybrid libraries are mixes of printed books and magazines, as well as electronic materials such as downloadable audio books, electronic journals, e-books, etc. Hybrid libraries are the new norm in most public and academic liberties (Rai, 2007).

The hybrid library is basically a combination of different types of library systems with different functions and services. Starting from collection to services, everything is of heterogeneous in nature. It hybrid library was designed to bring a range of technologies from different sources together in the context of a working library, and also to begin to explore integrated systems and services in both the electronic and print environments. The hybrid library should integrate access to different kinds of resources, using different technologies from the digital library world, and across different media. The name hybrid library is intended to reflect the transitional state of the library, which today can be neither fully print nor digital. Besides print collection, there are also the electronic resources in the library. Some housekeeping works are done through Library Management Software (LMS) whereas others are through traditional way; some collections are digitized and rest are printed. It is actually the transitional state between the traditional and automated libraries. The hybrid library tries to use the technologies available to bring things together into a library reflecting the best of both printed and electronic worlds.

The hybrid library (Pinfield et al., 1998; Brophy & Fisher 1998, Oppenheim & Smithson. 1999) is generally viewed by its proponents as a model in its own right, to be developed and improved, though it may be viewed by others as a transitional stage towards a truly digital library. This model represents the typical 'real world' situation, with pragmatic access to information from a range of media and formats, within an ideal of ever-closer integration and interoperability: it follows that most users will continue to be offered a mix of formats via a mix of delivery systems. The challenge for library managers is to create integrated services which provide a 'seamless' service to the user (Brophy & Fisher, 1998).

The hybrid library, since it has an element of physical provision and by implication a physical location in which these are stored and accessed, seems almost invariably to be an institutional model. In this way, it preserves the general concept of the traditional library, and, almost incidentally, retains the notation of the library as place; although there is considerable debate in the literature as to whether such an entity is properly regarded as primarily a place or a distributed process. Nevertheless, it seems clear that there will be a physical location associated with a hybrid (or gateway) library. The value of this should not be under-estimated, whether as the provision of space for student study in an educational institution, for community activities in a public library, or for knowledge management in a commercial organization, for which the physical conditions for knowledge sharing are being increasingly recognized as important. The hybrid library, for the same reasons, has an extended temporal existence. The position of the hybrid library with respect to the other library systems is shown in the figure-1.

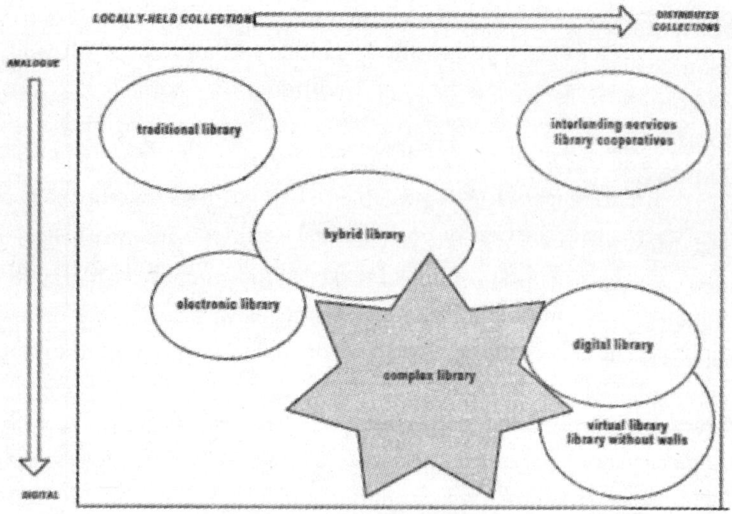

Fig. 1. Mapping different types of library models.
Source: Rowlands, I and Bawden, D

1.3.1.3. Electronic Library

Electronic library can be defined in many ways. Different terms such as "digital library", "electronic library" and "virtual library" are often used synonymously.

Electronic library encompasses the following components (Almisned, and ALanazi, 2007):

- **Database** : Collection or file of electronically stored data or unit records with software for the retrieval and manipulation of the data.
- **Downloading transaction** : Any procedure that aims to reproduce electronic data onto a local storage medium or printing facility.
- **Electronic library resources** : Every document in electronic form which needs special equipment to be used.
- **Electronic library services** : A service which is either supplied from local servers or accessible via networks.

Electronic Library envisages the library as a physical place, in which users may access digital resources one at a time. These electronic resources are selected, acquired, and made available for access and searching is very much the same way as traditional resources. This library has electronic resources in place of print documents of traditional library. This is a model of an incremental progress from traditional to digital, but is very much an automation of the status quo. It is unlikely that any library service would aspire to operate on such a model, and it may be regarded as a warning of the wrong way to digitise. As Rusbridge points out, however, absurd though it may be, it is the only model that can maintain anything like the traditional relationship with publishers, and the economic implications of this (Rowlands and Bawden, 1999).

1.3.1.4. Automated library

An automated library is one where a computer system is used to manage one or several of the library's key functions such as acquisitions, serials control, cataloging, circulation and the public access catalog. A library where access points and house keeping operations are computerized is called an automated library. The graphic records are still print-on-paper publication (Sharma, 2005). The library automation started when in the 80's the microcomputer became a useful tool for librarians who put to them to use for everything from word processing to reference, circulation and serials. Online Public Access Catalogs (OPAC) began to be used extensively in the 1980's. Libraries started to set-up and purchase their own computer systems as well as connect with other established library networks. Several software became available to librarians, such as spreadsheets and databases for help in library administration and information retrieval and dissemination. The introduction of CD-ROMs in the late 80s has drastically changed the library operations. The online services through CD-ROMs networking became available containing databases, software, and electronic information. Various online database services such as OCLC, DIALOG, and RLIN continued, however, in the early 90's the databases that were previously available online became available on CD-ROM, either in parts or in their entirety. Libraries could then gain information through a variety of options. The nineties gave rise to yet another era in library automation. The use of networks for e-mail, ftp, telnet, internet, and connections to on-line commercial systems has grown. It is now possible for users to connect to the libraries from their home or office. The World Wide Web, which had its official start date as April of 1993, is now becoming the fastest growing new provider of information. It is also possible, to connect to international library systems and information through the internet and with ever improving telecommunications. Expert systems and knowledge systems have become available in the 90s as both software and hardware capabilities have improved. The structure of the Automated Library is shown in the figure-2.

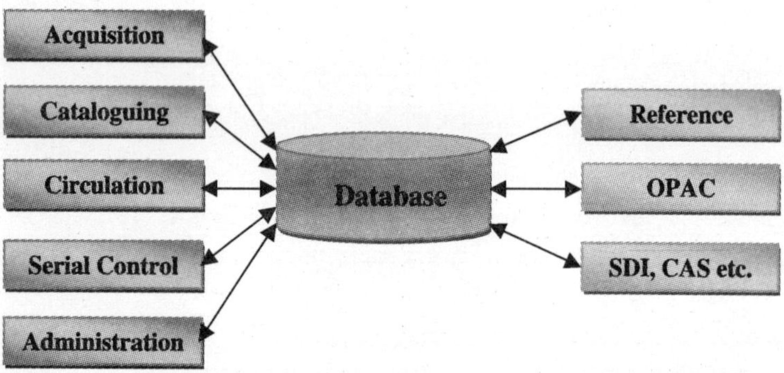

Fig. 2. Structure of the Automated Library System

1.3.1.5. Digital library

Digital library is nothing but the library in which a significant proportion of the resources are available in machine-readable format (as opposed to print or microform) accessible by means of computers. The digital content may be locally held or accessed remotely via computer networks (Reitz, 2008). In other words, a digital library is popularly viewed as an electronic version of a library where storage is in digital form, allowing direct communication to obtain material and copying it from a master version (Wiederhold, 1995).

Nowadays, due to awareness of education everywhere, the rate of reading of books has enormously increased. The efficiency of a college and university depends on its ability to manage information effectively, whether for educational, research, business or governmental purposes. Each time, we must rely on paper based library. The main concern of a paper oriented library is that it is not possible to have that many copies of books, journals etc. for cater to the demand of all students, lecturers, researchers at a time depending on this changing requirements. In real field scenarios this is not affordable by any library to keep all books with complete needed copies; implementation of Digital Libraries is the only way to bypass this problem.

The Digital Library is a critical technology for every person like students, lecturers, researchers, their guides as well as other persons willing to use that Digital Library. The Digital Library System refers to methods of gathering large amounts of information into digital form so that it can be stored, retrieved and manipulated by computer easily. Using DL, the retrieval of information is easy, with no limit of accessing. Various books, journals can be made available through this new technology based Digital Library (Jambhekar, 2011). Exactly what a digital library is and how it is to be organized have not yet been determined (Braude et al., 1995). It is not only digitization of physical resources, but also thoughtful organization of electronic collection for better access. Such an organization provides coherence to a massive amount of shared knowledge base.

Libraries, together with archives, have always been the primary institutions delegated to manage – collect, preserve and diffuse – human knowledge and culture. When advances in computer science allowed dealing with digital representation of documents dedicated to capture human knowledge and culture rather than printed ones, libraries are particularly involved in exploiting the potential of the digital revolution. Thus "digital libraries" soon became the term to indicate the digital counterpart of traditional libraries. However, digital library systems have greatly evolved since their early appearance. Today they have become complex networked systems able to support communication and collaboration among different worldwide distributed communities, dealing with "digital objects" comprising not only the digital counterpart video, programs and any other kind of multimedia objects a community may define as appropriate to its working and communication needs. been linear, coming from the contribution of many disciplines. This has created several conceptions of what a Digital Library is, each one influenced by the perspective or by the concrete needs it was designed to satisfy. Digital Libraries, which are now approximately twenty years old, is the history of a variety of different types of information systems that have been called "digital libraries". These systems are very heterogeneous in scope and functionality and their evolution does not follow a single path.

There are three domains in the conceptual framework of digital library (Figure-3). This relates the worlds of ideas and practice to a dynamic conception of the digital library with a strong temporal aspect (left-right) and informed by ideas rooted in Yates' notion of documents, technologies and work. We believe this framework summarizes many important issues in digital library research, not least the need for greater reflection and evaluation, a more transdisciplinary approach, and closer co-operation between academic, practitioner, user and policy-making communities. It should provide a valuable tool for understanding the nature of digital libraries and for comparing and analysis the results of research and the experience of practice.

Again from another angle the digital library framework may be viewed differently. Digital library system in true sense is actually the co-existence of many individual digital libraries or digital information system that may be: (a) ftp archive, (b) World Wide Web server, (c) on-line database, (d) a repository, etc.

The architectural components of digital libraries are of mainly four types namely user interface, repository, handle system and search system. The key components are shown in the figure- 4. They run on a variety of computer systems connected by a computer network, such as the Internet (Jana and Bhattacharya, 2009).

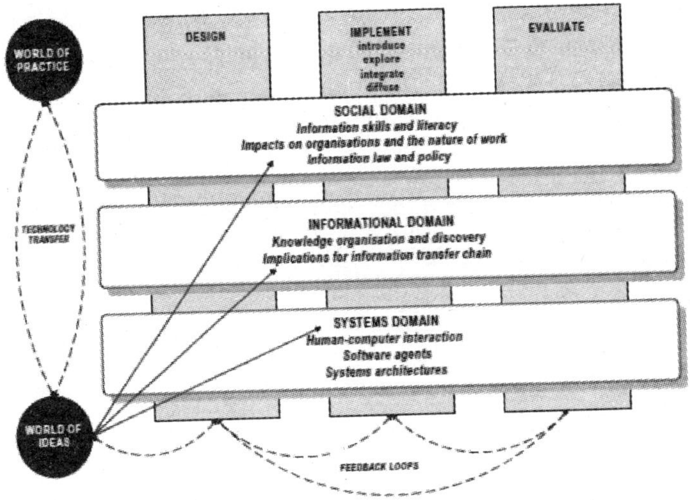

Fig. 3. Conceptual framework of digital library.
Source: Rowlands, I and Bawden, D

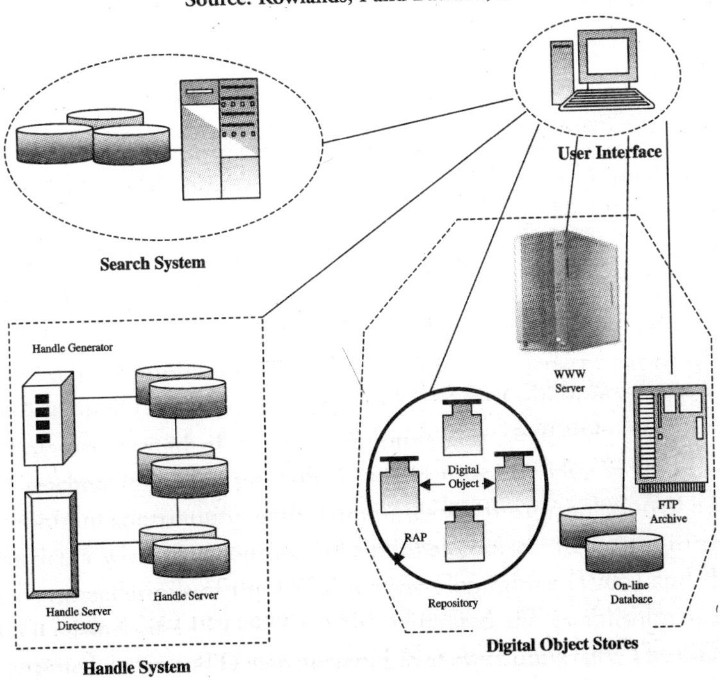

Fig. 4. Digital library framework

1. User interfaces : The interface through which any user can have their required digital information from digital stores is called user interface. There are two user interfaces: one for the users of the library, the other for the librarians and system administrators who manage the digital collections. Each user interface is working in two parts:

(a) *Browser* : A standard Internet **browser** like Netscape Navigator, Microsoft's Internet Explorer, Mozilla Firefox etc is used for the actual interactions with the user.

(b) *Client services* : It provides intermediary functions between the browser and the other parts of the system. The client services allow the user to decide where to search and what to retrieve; they interpret information structured as digital objects; they negotiate terms and conditions, manage relationships between digital objects, remember the state of the interaction, and convert among the protocols used by the various parts of the system.

2. Digital object stores : Information in the digital library can be stored in many types of store, as enumerated below:

(a) *FTP archive* : The archive where different digital files are stored and File Transfer Protocol is used for uploading and downloading the files over the internet. FTP works in the same way as HTTP for transferring Web pages from a server to a user's browser and SMTP for transferring electronic mail across the Internet. Like these technologies, FTP uses the Internet's TCP/IP protocols to enable data transfer.

(b) *World Wide Web server* : A WWW server is a program that runs 24hrs/day delivering files to requestors. Each WWW server on the Internet has its own name. The names often follow the www.organization.domain convention. Where organization is substituted by the organization's name or initials, and domain is determined by the type of organization (edu, com, org, net, etc.). Sub-units within the organization can add an extra item between the www. and the organization's name. Examples include www.sfsu.edu, www.journalism.sfsu.edu. The WWW Server program needs to be told where the documents to be served are located. Different web documents are stored in different WWW server. Each document has an URL. User can access these documents using this URL through web browser.

(c) *On-Line database* : An **online database** is a database accessible via a network, now generally the internet. It differs from a local database, held in an individual computer or its attached storage, such as a CD. Using the desktop computer, one can travel along the Internet to the server, and access the information (articles, pictures, etc.) stored in the database server. The information travels back to you, and is displayed on your computer monitor. You can usually save the information, ("download it to disk", or print it out), but the information is actually owned by the database producer, or "vendor". Service provider of online database connects the database of the database produces to the users through search system. The popular service providers are DIALOG, COMPUSERVE etc.

(d) *Repository* : The Repository addresses the need for uniformity by treating all forms of content as opaque, uniquely identified structures known as Digital Objects. By opaque, LIS professionals mean that neither the internal structure nor the semantics of Digital Objects are exposed. Essentially, from the Repository perspective, Digital Objects are atomic units, identifiable only by their unique names called handles. Repositories store and manage digital objects and other information associated with these objects. The interface to this repository is called the Repository Access Protocol (RAP). The RAP is responsible for the regulation of rights and permissions that need to be satisfied before a client can access a digital object within the repository. Repository is used mainly for storing valuable digital objects.

3. **Handle system** : Handles are general purpose identifiers that can be used to identify Internet resources, such as digital objects, over long periods of time and to manage materials stored in any

repository or database. Handle system is comprising of three components:

(a) ***Handle generator*** : Handle generator is responsible to create globally unique and unambiguous handles for digital objects before submitting these objects to the digital stores.

(b) ***Handle server*** : It stores the handles of the digital objects and the information associated with the location of the repository or store. During client's request, it interprets the handles to its corresponding locations and returns this information to the users.

(c) ***Handle server directory*** : It holds and manages the list of handle servers.

4. Search system : This is basically the database of indexes of digital objects having handles with different search options. The design of the digital library system assumes that there will be many indexes and catalogs that can be searched to discover digital information before retrieving it from a repository or store. These indexes must be compatible with Z 39.50 like standards to attain the interoperability with wide range of systems.

1.3.1.6. Virtual library

Virtual Library is the existence of library but without walls. It is based on the concept "Virtual Reality". When users will open the library interface, it will look like real library building with all the components of traditional library system in virtual reality environment. The users will get the flavor of traditional library but enjoy the facilities of digital library. But many authors use the term 'virtual library' synonymously to 'digital library' or 'electronic library'.

The access point as well as the graphic records are in electronic/ digital form when these electronic/digital libraries are connected via various networks, particularly the internet, this is called virtual library. A "library without walls" in which the collections do not exist on paper, microform, or other tangible form at a physical location but are electronically accessible in digital format via computer networks.

Such libraries exist only on a very limited scale, but in most traditional print-based libraries in the United States, catalogs and periodical indexes are available online, and some periodicals and reference works may be available in electronic full-text. Some libraries and library systems call themselves "virtual" because they offer online services; example: Colorado Virtual Library (Castelli, 2006).

1.3.1.7. Library 2.0

The Library 2.0 is basically the library having web 2.0 components or features. Library 2.0 is a loosely defined model for a modernized form of library service that reflects a transition within the library world in the way those services are delivered to users. The focus is on user-centered change and participation in the creation of content and community.

According to Miller (2005), "Library 2.0" is a term coined by Michael Casey on his LibrayCrunch blog. Though his writings on Library 2.0 are groundbreaking and in many ways authoritative, Casey (2006) defines the term very broadly, arguing it applies beyond technological innovation and service. In addition to Casey, other blogging librarians have begun conceptually exploring what Library 2.0 might mean, and because of this disparate discussion with very wide parameters, there is some controversy over the definition and relative importance of the term. Due to the nature of this controversy Lawson (2006), Peek (2005), and Tebbutt (2006) explore and begin to adequately rectify, and Crawford (2006) provides a very thorough account of the ambiguity and confusion surrounding the term, partially suggesting that there is nothing inherently novel about the idea.

A theory for Library 2.0 could be understood to have these four essential elements: (Maness, 2006).

- **It is user-centered.** Users participate in the creation of the content and services they view within the library's web-presence, OPAC, etc. The consumption and creation of content is dynamic, and thus the roles of librarian and user are not always clear.

- **It provides a multi-media experience.** Both the collections and services of Library 2.0 contain video and audio components. While this is not often cited as a function of Library 2.0, it is here suggested that it should be.
- **It is socially rich.** The library's web-presence includes users' presence. There are both synchronous (e.g. IM) and asynchronous (e.g. wikis) ways for users to communicate with one another and with librarians.
- **It is communally innovative.** This is perhaps the single most important aspect of Library 2.0. It rests on the foundation of libraries as a community service, but understands that as communities change, libraries must not only change with them, and they must allow users to change the library. It seeks to continually change its services, to find new ways to allow communities, not just individuals to seek, find, and utilize information.

The concept of Library 2.0 borrows from that of Business 2.0 and Web 2.0 and follows some of the same underlying philosophies. Library 2.0 model gives library users a participatory role in the services libraries offer and the way they are used. Customers, should they desire, will be able to tailor library services to best meet their own needs. This can be done electronically, such as through the personalization of library web pages, or physically through new service options such as allowing customers to call impromptu book talks or discussion groups. Such collaborative efforts require librarians to develop a more intensive routine of soliciting customer response and regularly evaluating and updating services (Casey, 2006).

1.3.1.8. Global library

Friedman (2006) stated the globalization as the interweaving of markets, technology, information systems and telecommunications systems in a way that is shrinking and flattening the world. Globalization enables us to go around the world farther, faster, deeper, and cheaper than ever before, and vise versa. Rikowski (2005) expounds four contradictory dimensions in which globalization manifests. The first dimension is the cultural dimension. In globalization, the diversity of various cultures in the world as well as the challenge of homogenizing different cultures must be acknowledged. The second dimension addresses the vanishing of national power in the global economy, with the emergence of so many transnational organizations, such as the World Bank and the International Monetary Fund. These transnational organizations set up the standards of the field in the world and greatly influence the national organizations. The third dimension is the capital's expansion, which illustrates the individual lives in the global market. The last but the most important dimension is the global labor value. With globalization, employers can hire the best value labor across the world to maximize profit. These four contradictory dimensions demonstrate that globalization brings opportunities as well as challenges to us.

Not long ago, "the end of stand-alone library" was an evil omen. Now it seems that "the end of local library" might come soon, as the beginning of the "global library" is on the horizon. Globalization, the most progressive global movement since the Industrial Revolution, has brought an enormous impact to every single continent and every single industry. As libraries are increasingly obtaining resources from and providing services to users all across the world, a new model of library services and operations emerges, which is referred to as the Global Library (GL).

The Global Library can be defined with the following key characteristics. It is globally accessible in either virtual or physical library environment;

(1) provides global users with 24x7 services;

(2) hosts global-focused library collections and resources;

(3) employs global talents;

(4) operates globally, even though the headquarters are in a home country;

(5) is actively engaged in library-related activities for global communities.

The benefits of the Global Library:

- Integration of resources
- Equal access to local and global resources
- Maximized productivity and minimized operational cost
- Leverage the local and specialized talents
- Promotion of international library standards and preservation of local civilization and culture as well

The challenges of the Global Library:

- Preservation of the local culture
- Balance of various cultures in management
- Understanding of local religion, ideology, political systems, etc.
- Requirement of new managerial skill sets in a global and cross-cultural management environment

Some existing examples of the global library or global library-like services: OCLC virtual reference QuestionPoint (http://www.oclc.org/questionpoint/about/default.htm); Global distance education with library services (http://www.logintolearn.com/nextdistance.html); Global Library Initiative (http://www.globallibrary.org/en/index.php); Multi-National Corporate (MNC) global library services (http://www.online-information.co.uk/2004proceedings/thursam/heye_d.pdf).

1.3.1.9. Social systems as competitors to libraries

Many social systems in digital age are acting as information disseminator like library. So if we are not to be left high and dry we need to develop a Libraries 2.0 to match Web 2.0 and that in turn will be dependent on our ability to focus on and determine the needs of the new user and not the technologies which they have currently adopted. These Web 2.0 spaces form big hubs where users congregate and on which services can be built. The web 2.0 in the present time is 'of the users, by the users and for the users', where users can generate information, edit it and retrieve it as and when required.

The big upsurge in social networking services is based on blogs, wikis: instant messaging and other tools which are creating new spaces where services are being built, spaces which are quite foreign to libraries. Youtube acquired twenty million users a month in eighteen months and they watch one hundred million video clips a day. Youtube now been taken over by Google is a perfect example of aggregation. Myspace has one hundred million users and the number is growing by 240,000 a day, while Google receives one billion requests a day.

Unlike social-networking sites such as LinkedIn and Friendster, which concentrate on developing relationships, social sites such as del.icio.us, 43Things and Flickr focus their attention on organizing data. Users organize their own or other's data in the public sphere and the social, or community, aspects arise from there as users share and seek out like-minded individuals. And if even classification is under threat, what is left?

These services are described on their own websites in simple jargon free attractive ways. For example, "The Semantic Web is about two things. It is about common formats for interchange of data, where on the original Web we only had interchange of documents. Also it is about language for recording how the data relates to real world objects. That allows a person, or a machine, to start off in one database, and then move through an unending set of databases which are connected not by wires but by being about the same thing." Wikipedia describes how folksonomies develop in internet-mediated social environments, users can discover (generally) who created a given folksonomy tag, and see the other tags that this person created. In this way, folksonomy users often discover the tag sets of another user who tends to interpret and tag content in a way that makes sense to them. The result, often, is an immediate and rewarding gain in the user's capacity to find related content. Part of the appeal of folksonomy is its inherent subversiveness: faced with the dreadful performance of the search tools that web sites typically provide, folksonomies can be seen as a rejection of the search engine status quo in favor of tools that are both created by the community and beneficial to the community and as to place, most Starbuck's café's provide superior wireless internet access to most libraries.

It is then easy to tabulate where digital natives go to meet their information needs instead of the library. But libraries are great survivors and there are areas where the profession can claim to have relevant skills. Ironically these are best seen as developments and re-branding of traditional skills.

Table 1. Differences among Traditional Library, Web 2.0 World and Library 2.0 World

Traditional Library	*Web 2.0 World*	*Library 2.0 World*
Cataloguing	Automated metadata, del.icio.us	Metadata
Classification	Folksonomies and the semantic web	Locally provided and relevant folksonomy
Acquisitions	e-bay, Paypal, Amazon and Abebooks	E-archives, e-data and quality assurance
Reference	Yahoo Answers and Wikipedia	Branded links to trusted resources
Preservation	Digital Archives and repositories	Institutional repository
User Instruction	Chatrooms	Moderate chatroom
Working space	Bedroom and Starbucks with a laptop	Wired campus and 24-hour workspace
Collections	Youtube, Flickr, Institutional Repositories, Open Access	Aggregation of unique content with other libraries
Professional judgment	The wisdom of crowds	Teaching retrieval skills

1.3.2. Libraries on the basis of objectives and nature of users

Libraries can be distinguished on the basis of its objectives and nature of users also. Gupta (2011) has given elaborate note of different types libraries on the basis of these criteria's.

1.3.2.1. National Library

The concept of national libraries is a recent development dating back to a few centuries. This development has been a feature of socio-economic, culture and scientific advancements in the western industrially advanced countries. The growth and advancement of such libraries has been a conspicuous feature of the intellectual and cultural development of a country. Not only have they grown in size, particularly in the last half a century, they have also expanded in multifold dimensions, tending to develop into a network of national libraries.

Definition : The ALA *Glossary of Library Terms,* simply defines, the National Library as "a library maintained by a Nation". A more comprehensive definition of a National Library was attempted by UNESCO, at its 16th session of the General Conference held in 1970, when UNESCO made "Recommendations Concerning International Standardization of Library Statistics". The following definition of the National Library occurs in this document;

Libraries which, irrespective of their title, are responsible for-

(1) Acquiring and conserving copies of all significant publications publishcd in the country;

(2) Functioning as a 'depository' library, whether by law or under other arrangements.

They will also normally perform some of the following functions:

a. produce a national bibliography,

b. hold and keep up-to-date a large representative collection or foreign literature, including books about the country;

c. act as a national bibliographical information centre;

d. compile union catalogues

e. publish retrospective bibliographies..:."

A **National Library** keeps all documents of and about a nation under some legal provision and thus represents publications of and about the whole nation.

Objectives : A National Library works with the following objectives:

(1) It provides leadership among the nation's libraries;

(2) It procures nation's all literary output under legal provision as well as the foreign literature about that nation and serve as a permanent national depository

(3) It works as a depository house for the said heritage by preserving it;

(4) It disseminates information about the stored and procured literary wealth through different publications and services;

(5) It works as a national referral and bibliographic exchange centre;

(6) It coordinates with the other libraries in a country to develop a national library system; and

(7) It provides service to government.

Functions of National Library

- It works as a national depository library for all literary work published in the country;
- It freely collects copies of all published material in the country through legal deposits, gifts or exchange;
- It collects and preserve select manuscripts and such other archival records of national relevance and importance;
- It also procures foreign publications about the country; and by the authors of Indian origin living abroad;
- It compiles national bibliographies to disseminate information about literary output of the country;
- It works as an apex body of the national library system and coordinates with other libraries in the country;
- It develops and maintains different bibliographic databases and works as a national bibliographic centre;
- It also exchanges data and documents at national and international level;
- It produces national union catalogues, current, retrospective and subject bibliographies;
- It makes provision for practical training of library professionals;
- It acquires and maintains documents about the country or its people or activities, published outside the country by any national or in any language or form;

- It also keeps photocopy collection of available documents for national and international library lending;
- It provides reading, lending, consulting facilities to researchers, writers and other users;
- It works as a national referral centre of authentic information for all literary work of the country and responds to all national and international queries from individuals as well as from private and government organizations.
- It collects and preserve select manuscripts and such other archival records of national relevance and importance;
- It provides inter-library lending and serving as a national and international, inter-library loan centres;
- It provides photocopying services, including the preparation of slides, overhead transparencies and other facilities to scholars, researchers and others;
- It compiles of retrospective or current bibliographies on various subjects in anticipation of or on request.
- It conserves the national intellectual and cultural heritage for the benefit of the country as a whole
- It collects foreign documents for which there may be demand from the people of the country;
- It also collects and preserve specialized materials such as books for the blind, dramatic compositions, engravings, medals, music compositions, cinematic films, photographs, sound recordings, etc., if these materials are not being collected by other agencies;
- It provides facilities for reading, consulting, etc., on the premises, including research alcoves/rooms for serious readers such as researchers; scholars and writers.

Types of the National Library

Table 2. Types of the National Library

Types	*Functions*	*Examples*
Comprehensive	All functions	National Library of Canada
By Functions	Lending	British Library Lending Division (Formerly National Lending Library for Science and technology)
By Subject	Agriculture	National Agriculture Library, USA
	Medicine	National Medical Library, India
	Science	National Science Library. India
	Scientific & Technical	Technical Library USSR
By special groups	Blind,	National Library for the Blind, UK
	Legislators	National Diet Library, Japan
Sub-National serving a geographical area or cultural group	Area/State/cultural group	National Library of Wales National Libraries of Serbia, USSR National Library of Scotland
Sharing	Sharing functions	State and University of Aarhus, Denmark

(IGNOU, 1999c)

1.3.2.2. Public Library

Public libraries serve communities of all sizes and types. Wherever you live, there's bound to be a local public library nearby! As the name implies, public libraries serve the general public, "from cradle to grave" as more than one public librarian has been heard to say. Public libraries often have departments that focus on areas of service, such as youth, teens and adults.

Definition : According to UNESCO Public Library Manifesto 1949 which was revised in 1972, a public library is-

(1) established under the "clear mandate of law";

(2) maintained wholly from "public fund";

(3) levies no "direct charge" (fees) from its users for any of its services;

(4) open "for free and equal " use by all members of the community irrespective of race, colour, caste, creed, religion, age, sex, nationality, language, status or level of educational attainments;

(5) the local gateway to knowledge, provides a basic condition for lifelong learning, independent decision making and cultural development of the individual and social groups;

(6) an essential agent for the fostering of peace and spiritual welfare through the minds of men and women.

According to Dr.S.R.Ranganathan, Public Library is "a public institution or establishment charged with the care of collection of books and the duty of making them accessible to those who require the use of them." This definition describes two functions of a library:

(1) the care of a collection of books means protection and preservation of collection.

(2) to make them accessible in real sense so that the right person can get right information at the right time.

In other words, a Public Library is a social institution established by law, financed by public fund, open for all without any discrimination, for general and free diffusion of knowledge and information in the community. It is the obligation of government to establish a public library system throughout the country at national, state and local levels. Besides this, the rural and suburban areas should also be covered by branch and mobile libraries.

Key Missions of Public Library

The UNESCO, in its public library manifesto, for the first time spelled out the key missions which relate to information, literacy, education and culture and should be at the core of public library services:

- providing access to cultural expressions of all performing arts;
- fostering inter-cultural dialogue and favouring cultural diversity;
- supporting the oral tradition;

- ensuring access for citizens to all sorts of community information;
- providing adequate information services to local enterprises, associations and interest groups;
- facilitating the development of information and computer literacy skills;
- supporting and participating, in literacy activities and programmes for all age groups, and initiating such activities.

Objectives : The objectives of a public library are associated with its parent body i.e. community and its duty are to cater to the information and recreational needs of its users i.e. community members. (IGNOU, 1999d).

The main objectives of a public library are as follows:

1. To provide services free of cost or at nominal rates to each member of the society without any discrimination;
2. To create and strengthen reading skills and habits in children from an early age;
3. To support both individual and self conducted education as well as formal education;
4. To provide opportunities for personal creative development;
5. To stimulate the imagination and creativity of children and young people;
6. To promote awareness of cultural heritage, appreciation of the arts, scientific achievements and innovations;
7. To provide up-to-date and authentic information on all subjects;
8. To provide a harmless and elevating use of leisure;
9. To be responsible for preservation and development of cultural and antiquarian heritage of the community.
10. To provide access to cultural expressions of all performing arts;
11. To foster inter-cultural dialogue and favouring cultural diversity;

12. To support the oral tradition;
13. To ensure access for citizens to all sorts of community information;
14. To provide adequate information services to local enterprises, associations and interest groups;
15. To facilitate the development of information and computer literacy skills;
16. To support and participate, in literacy activities and programmes for all age groups, and initiating such activities, if necessary.

Functions : A modern public library performs different functions in the society to achieve its objectives and works as:

A) Information Dissemination Centre

For this purpose it collects, processes and then disseminates up-to-date and authentic information on all subjects according to the information needs of the local community. It develops collection on the basis of educational level, literacy rate, age groups, nature of occupation, profession, language, cultural habits and reading interest etc. of the local population to provide barrier-free information.

B) Life Long Learning Centre

(1) It works like a life long learning centre and each and every person of the community is a life member of this centre. Therefore it is known as a public university or a library of public university.

(2) This provides a strong base for adult education programmes. To cultivate reading habits among children at an early age, it makes provision for special collections or separate section or wing for them in the library premises.

(3) It acquires documents on all subjects to provide support system for all modes of education systems especially for adult education, non-formal, and self-education systems.

(4) It provides latest information in different disciplines to facilitate

the users to improve and develop their skills and competency by self learning.

C) Community's Intellectual Centre

A public library works as a common platform to provoke and stimulate the intellectual, educational, social and spiritual thinking of the community. By organizing seminars, debates, exhibitions, lectures etc. it tries to involve each and every person of the society in such activities so that they can exchange their ideas, experiences, suggestions etc. and thus develop their interest to perform as an active part of the society. It enhances mutual understanding among the people and makes them efficient to solve the social and local problems on their own.

D) Recreation Centre

A public library performs this function also. It provides refreshment for man's spirit by the provision of documents like fiction, audiovisuals etc. for relaxation, pleasure and entertainment. The cultural programmes organized by the public library also give support to this function. It encourages healthy recreation and constructive use of leisure time of its users.

E) Community's Cultural Hub

A public library works as a cultural center also. It promotes different cultural activities of that locality by organizing cultural programmes such as dramas, music concerts, folk dances, puppet shows etc. in its premises. These programmes provide entertainment as well as develop communal harmony in the society. It also promotes awareness of cultural heritage, appreciation of the arts, scientific achievements and innovations and provides access to cultural expressions of all performing arts. It helps in fostering inter-cultural dialogue by favoring cultural diversity. It collects and preserves material relating to the history and culture of its area. It conserves culture and art and also makes its further transmission.

F) Instrument of Social Change

It works as an effective instrument to create awareness in the society. By organizing seminars, debates, workshops, exhibitions etc. it creates awareness regarding contemporary political and social issues and stigmas in the society. With the help of suitable documents it influences the attitude of public in combating prejudicial treatment of certain groups, thus removes barriers between groups of people. It also works as a catalyst by awakening masses at the grass root level with the power of knowledge.

G) Establishment of Democracy

A public library represents the real meaning of democracy. By providing equal access to all community members without any bias it enhances equality and social justice, promotes intellectual freedom and advancement of knowledge, generates in the young generation a sense of purposefulness dedication and confidence in themselves and faith in democracy's future. It works as a platform in the community for open and fruitful discussions, to have healthy dialogues with each other and to share their views and experiences on some common problems. This increases respect for other religions and faiths. It also helps to bring all the people in to the main stream of the society with their active participation. Through general diffusion of knowledge it creates enlightened citizen.

1.3.2.3. Academic Library

Academic libraries are considered to be the centres of academic institutions, and must support teaching, research, and other academic programmes. The situation in academic libraries of India is the same as that of academic libraries the world over; however, Indian libraries provided maximum information with limited resources. The academic libraries support learning, teaching, research and other educational functions appropriate to their parent institutions (IGNOU, 1999a).

The National Knowledge Commission was set up by the Government of India on 13th June 2005 with a time-frame of three years, from 2nd October 2005 to 2nd October 2008. As a high-level advisory body to the Prime Minister of India, the National Knowledge Commission was given a mandate to guide policy and direct reforms, focusing on certain key areas such as education, science and technology, agriculture, industry, e-governance etc. Easy access to knowledge, creation and preservation of knowledge systems, dissemination of knowledge and better knowledge services are core concerns of the Commission (*http://www.knowledgecommission.gov.in/about/default.asp*).

The Commission envisaged the future road map for the growth and development of academic libraries by imbibing core issues such as, set up a national commission on libraries, prepare a national census of all libraries, revamp LIS education, training and research facilities, re-assess staffing of libraries, set up a central library fund, modernize library management, encourage greater community participation in library management, promote information communication technology applications in all libraries, facilitate donation and maintenance of private collections, and encourage public private partnerships in LIS development, etc. (*http://www.knowledgecommission.gov.in/recommendations/libraries.asp*).

An Academic Library has been defined as: "a library which is associated or attached with any educational institution to support its educational programmes". Academic library is an integral part of formal education system which provides time bound education from primary school level to university level. An academic library works as a base for teaching, learning, research etc.

We can categorize academic libraries in to following three categories-

1. School Library
2. College Library
3. University Library.

1.3.2.3.1. School Library

Education is a process of learning, with the aim to develop the capabilities in the people at all levels. The story of India's educational achievements is one of mixed success. On the down side, India has 22 per cent of the world's population but 46 per cent of the world's illiterates, and is home to a high proportion of the world's out of school children and youth. On the positive side, it has made encouraging progress in recent years in raising schooling participation. In the academic process schools, colleges and universities play a vital role. The school authorities do build a variety of facilities to operate different functions of the school in order to meet the requirements of its students. One of the most important facilities is the provision of a modern library and its expanded services. In recent decades, libraries have been considered not merely a facility but as the chief instrument of learning in all its dimensions. Libraries could help students both in their academic and non-academic pursuits.

Definition : A library associated or connected with a school and used by the students, teachers and staff of that school is called a School library.

Objectives : A school library has the following objectives (IGNOU, 1999a):

1. It supports all educational programmes of the school;
2. It cultivates reading habits in school children;
3. It develops their interest to use the library for their overall development;
4. It inculcates the habit of seeking help of additional sources other than text books;
5. It develops self-learning skills of students;
6. It nurtures good moral values and principles in the children;
7. It cultivates a feeling of respect and love for nation and its culture in the students;
8. It helps teachers to improve their teaching expertise;
9. It provides healthy material for recreational and entertainment purpose to students, teachers and staff members;
10. It keeps the teachers and management informed with the latest updates in education sector.

Functions : To achieve the above said objectives a school library performs the following functions-

1. It provides suitable documents and information helpful in educational programmes and extracurricular activities of the school;
2. It makes available text books and other additional reading material for all subjects as per the requirement of teachers and students;
3. It procures handy documents, illustrated picture books with bold and large fonts to create the interest of children in reading.
4. It procures latest teaching learning material in the form of books, CD, audio-visuals etc. to improve the teaching skills of teachers.
5. It keeps reference books, dictionaries, year books, directories, encyclopedias, travel books etc. so that students and teachers can get help of these other than the text books.
6. It also keeps some books on easy self learning like how to use computer, to develop the learning skills of students.
7. It makes available biographies, autobiographies of freedom fighters and other national and international personalities to develop respect and love for nation and humanity.
8. It procures magazines like Nandan, Chmpak, India Today, Readers Digest etc., different newspapers, and other light reading material like fiction books, general knowledge books, poetry books, short animated films, documentaries etc. for healthy recreation and entertainment purpose of students, teachers and school staff.
9. It provides books of simple and meaningful stories of classics, panchtantra, animals and birds to give moral values and ethics to children.
10. It also procures bulletins, journals etc. on different subjects and various aspects of education to keep the teachers and school management updated in their respective areas.

1.3.2.3.2. College Library

College plays an important role in the academic educational process. College education provides a totally different environment for boys and girls who go for higher studies. Usually the classes comprise a large number of students and unlike school education, the students of college get much less individual attention from the teachers. The students, therefore, have to end much more on self-learning. Therefore, the college library is the automatic choice for students to supplement their class room teaching (IGNOU, BLIS paper-1, unit-6). The College libraries in India have a significant role to play in higher education. Majority of the undergraduate students, i.e., 88.5 per cent and graduate students, i.e., 53 per cent, attend these colleges (Kipp and Kipp, 1961). When India attained Independence many among the 533 affiliated colleges (Sharma, 1986) did not have their own libraries, but at present, every college in the country has a library. Majority of the college libraries do not have proper facilities to meet the needs of their users. Their collections are not up-to-date, budgets are very inadequate and limited, and a large number of them are single libraries. In many colleges, there is neither a library hall nor a sufficient room, not to think of a separate building for the library. Any unused room, quite often somewhere out of sight, would be considered adequate to house a few shelves of books. And in most college libraries there is complete darkness even during the day time, as the windows are closed out of fear that the books may be stolen (Kumar, 1978). The college libraries are open only six to eight hours a day. Many do not have any qualified librarian on their staff and have closed stacks only (Deshpande, 1978). The college library system requires some essential components:

- a collection of books and other learning and teaching material;
- the user community, comprising students, teachers, the college management and others getting standard library services;
- physical facilities like building, furniture, equipment;
- professional staff for the library;
- the college management finance and budget.

Definition : A library attached or associated with a college and used by teachers, students and staff of the college is known as College Library.

Objectives : The objectives of a college library are as follows:

- It helps in all educational and instructional programmes of the college;
- It develops a habit of deep and advanced studies of subjects beyond the text books of subjects, in students;
- It enhances the understanding of different subjects or disciplines among students;
- It prepares the students as an intelligent, aware, informative and enlightened person to play the role of a responsible citizen;
- It assists the research work and lays down the initiative base for research work in students;
- It informs the teachers with latest up-dates in their respective subject area;
- It provides healthy entertainment material to its users;

Functions : To achieve its objectives a college library performs the following functions:

1. In order to help in all educational and instructional programmes of the college it develops its collection by acquiring different documents like textbooks, audiovisuals etc. related to various courses offered by the college ;
2. It also procures a good amount of more advanced books other than text books on different subjects to develop a habit of deep and advanced studies among college students.
3. It acquires reference books such as encyclopedias and other books on each and every aspect of different subjects to enhance the understanding of subjects among students on their own besides class-room teaching and text-books
4. To prepare the students for different professions and occupations and to develop their skills it procures self learning material, competitive exam books etc. ;

5. It procures newspapers, weekly and monthly magazines on current events, general knowledge books etc. to make aware its users about their surroundings.
6. It subscribes to useful journals, research bulletins on different subjects as per the recommendations of faculty (teachers) for research work and to keep the teachers abreast with the latest in their disciplines;
7. If some document is not available in the library it brings it on inter-library loan on demand of its users.
8. It also provides light reading material like fiction, biographies, magazines, travel book guides, audio-visuals etc. to give healthy leisure time to its users;
9. It procures general reference books such as dictionaries, directories, encyclopedias, yearbooks as well as some subject specific reference books.
10. To make library and its use more accessible and easy it makes proper classification, cataloguing, shelf arrangement, display of new arrivals and provides services like bibliographical, indexing, abstracting etc.
11. It provides orientation training to its new users to use the library and disseminate information time to time regarding new library services and latest books.

1.3.2.3.3. University Library

University libraries all over the world have their own place of importance in the scheme of higher learning. Libraries are not only repositories of knowledge but also dispensers of such knowledge. There is no doubt that where libraries of universities and institutions of higher learning are ignored or not given due recognition, the country as a whole suffers because the standards of study, teaching and research very heavily depend upon the qualitative and quantitative service rendered by the university libraries. The Radhakrishnan Commission (1948-49) expressed that "the library is the heart of all the university's work, directly so, as regards its research work and indirectly as regards its educational work, which derives its life from research. Scientific research needs the library as well as its laboratories while for humanistic research the library is both library and the laboratory in one. Both for humanistic and scientific studies, a first class library is essential in a university" (India, 1949).

The growth of university libraries since Independence can be seen in respect of the initiatives taken by the Central Government considering the vital importance of higher education and role of libraries in the educational development, commitment to fulfill the demand of higher education, and the foundation of the UGC in 1953 by an Act of Parliament. The Radhakrishnan Commission (1948) recognized the value and importance of a well equipped and organized library system and its role in higher education. It had found many drawbacks and pitfalls in the university libraries and had made many recommendations for the improvement of library facilities. The Ranganathan Committee, appointed by the UGC in 1957, made some outstanding recommendations, which included standards for library building, collection development, staff and services and furniture etc. These recommendations were accepted by the UGC and forwarded for implementation. The Kothari Commission also made valuable recommendations for this purpose, but the role of the University Grants Commission deserves special mention, because it has played a vital role by "regularly providing appropriate grants and funds to all universities for development of libraries, to purchase books and journals, construction of new library buildings and for library equipment and furniture" (Ojha, 1980).

A library attached or associated with a university and used by students, teachers, researchers, administrative staff etc. of the university as well as by the other research workers, alumni outside the university is known as university library. It is also known as the heart of university. It works like an axis of all educational and research activities in all disciplines. According to Dr. Krishan Kumar "a university library is a part of a university set up. Therefore, it exists to serve the objectives of its parent organization. Every library programme must support university's total programme. In other words, a university library should aim to advance the functions of its university. It should reflect character of the university". He also states that the major distinction between a college library and university library is that a university library lays emphasis mainly upon research. Thus we find that research is a major objective of a university library. In others words, it circulates knowledge to generate new knowledge.

Objectives : A University Library has the following objectives:

- To provide facilities for all teaching, learning, educational and research programmes of the university;
- To cater to the information needs of teachers, students, researchers associated with the university;
- It provides facilities to its users for intellectual development which is a power of acquiring ideas through individual efforts;
- It conserves knowledge;
- By putting knowledge to use for research purpose it makes extension of knowledge;
- By providing latest knowledge to teachers in their field for effective teaching it makes transmission of knowledge possible.

Functions : The universally recognized basic functions performed by a University Library are:

1. By procuring comprehensive range of documents including books, manuscripts, journals, magazines, newspapers etc. on varied subjects, it conserves knowledge and ideas.
2. By processing the procured documents with the help of classification, cataloguing, proper shelf arrangements it gives easy and open access to knowledge to its users;
3. In order to organize huge collection of documents it keeps them in different sections on the basis of their categorization like text book section, reference section, journal section, thesis section etc.;
4. It provides facility of inter-library loan to its users if document desired by user is not available in the library;

5. A modern university library interacts with different information networks to give easy access to e-resources/ data to more users so that they could access the desired information even from their workplace. For example in India university libraries use the facility of INFLIBNET for the same purpose ;
6. It also provides entertainment and healthy leisure to users by providing different newspapers, magazines, short story books, fiction, internet facility etc.
7. It gives the user orientation training to new enrolled users to make them feel at home and to acquaint them with the library system so that they could make maximum use of library services;
8. With the help of display of new arrivals, book exhibitions, information bulletins about new library services etc. it keeps the users updated with the library activities;
9. It provides reference service through reference section to establish a contact between the right reader and the right document in a personal way to attract more users;

1.3.2.4. Special Library

In 20th century with the development of industrial, technological and scientific advances the concept of special libraries came in to existence. The growing need for specialized information for further development and research came to play a vital role in the expansion of special libraries. Special libraries are formed in research and development ' establishments, government departments, directorates, industrial and business undertakings, learned societies and professional associations, trade and business associations, hospitals and health services, social and welfare organisations, museums, national gallery of arts; etc. However special libraries are also established to serve a particular group of users or specialists working on a subject or a group of subjects or on a particular type of documents, etc. (IGNOU, 1999e).

Definition : According to the Special Library Association's *Association Fact Sheet,* "SLA represents information professionals who collect, analyze, evaluate, package and disseminate information to facilitate strategic decision-making. SLA's members work for corporations, private companies, government agencies, not-for-profit organizations, technical and academic institutions, museums, law firms, and medical facilities."

Now, this seems like a broad description, but special librarianship is a broad field. As defined by the Special Libraries Association, a special library is a place where information is evaluated, analyzed, organized, packaged, and presented in a manner that "maximizes its usefulness." Many definitions of special libraries concern themselves with where to find a special library and not particularly with defining what they do.

According to American Library Association (ALA) glossary of library and information science- Special Library is "a library established, supported and administered by a business firm, private corporation, association, government agency or other special interest group or agency to meet the information needs of its members or staff in pursuing the goals of the organistion. Scope of collections and services is limited to the subject interest of the host or parent organization". In other words, special library collects updated and comprehensive information on the subject concerned with the parent organization and disseminate this information promptly to the people associated with the organization on demand and in anticipation.

Objectives : The main objectives of a special library are as follows:

1. It serves the information needs of its parent body;
2. It disseminates updated and significant information in the concerned field;
3. It gives pinpointed information promptly;
4. It provides desired information to its users on demand and mostly in anticipation;
5. The users also get new ideas and inspiration to initiate new projects.

Functions : A special library performs primarily the following functions:

1. It selects and procures documents and other sources of relevant information;
2. It processes the procured information or documents with the help of classification, cataloguing, shelf arrangements etc. to make them easily available for the users;
3. It subscribes to a good number of journals related to its area;
4. It provides indexing, abstracting and extracting services to the users to save their time;
5. It provides reference services to the users by telephone, by post or by e-mail;
6. It gives Current Awareness Service (CAS) regarding new arrivals and latest services to the users;
7. It provides Selective Dissemination of Information (SDI) service to the users as per their subject interest and requirement;
8. It also gives document delivery service to its users at their doorstep;
9. It brings out library bulletins weekly/fortnightly/monthly to keep the users up to date with latest information;
10. It performs translation services to provide the desired information to the users in their convenient language.
11. It also provides intranet as well as internet facility to the users in order to access the library collection and catalogues at their desktop;
12. It responds to the reference queries and make retrospective search of literature as per the users' demand;
13. It compiles bibliographies, union catalogues, documentation lists, newspaper- clippings, accession lists etc. to save the time of its users;
14. It provides Inter Library Loan (ILL) facility to the users;
15. It gives user orientation training through personal interaction

with users and by library brochure and pamphlets to make the users familiar with the library collection and services.

16. It prepares accession lists, bulletins, news-letters; summaries, hand-books or manuals;

Types : There is a wide variety, but we can break down special libraries in to common categories by subject matter. This list was synthesized using a combination of resources from the Catholic University of America, the SLA and the University of South Carolina College of Library and Information Science. (LIS 6010 Blog, 2009).

- Art Library
- Botanical Library
- Corporate Library
- Law Library
- Local History Library
- Map Library
- Medical Library
- Military Library
- Map Library
- Museum Library
- Music Library
- News Library
- Nonprofit Organization Library
- Personal Library (working for someone with an unusual amount of money and collections)

Examples:

1. **National Library for the Blind**: It deals with special kind of documents i.e. Braille and audio books and also with special user group i.e. persons with visual impairment or blind.

2. **Library of Supreme Court of India:** It keeps major collection of court cases and decisions which are mainly used by lawyers and judges, thus the user group is also of a special kind.

3. Library of Indian Standards Institute (ISI): It mainly keeps patents which are special type of document and used by some special user group and related to some specific field or area.

1.3.3. Libraries on the basis of mode of access to the documents

1.3.3.1 Open Access Library

Open access library is nothing but the library where users are able to enter into the library and can reach book shelves directly. This system plays a vital role in the maximum use of library materials as users can freely brows all books, selects from the library shelf and know about the library collection widely. Long days ago McColvin (1951) provides a detailed idea regarding open access system in the library.

1. The Open Access System has been used for many years throughout Great Britain, the United States, Sweden, Norway, Denmark and elsewhere. In Open Access libraries the public are allowed to go to the shelves to select for themselves the books they wish to read, and also to examine those that are available, to browse, to learn about the varied materials that are provided. The Open Access system is found in both Lending and Reference Departments but in these notes we are chiefly concerned with the former.

2. The Advantages of open Access System many but the most important are :

(a) Unless readers can handle the books, it is impossible for them to choose those which, will best suit their purposes, be best adopted to their reading abilities and give them the maximum benefit and enjoyment. Where the open access system is not in operation, readers must rely either upon catalogues or the assistance of staff and in either case must suffer many disappointments and limitations; for the best, catalogues can give little idea of how a particular book will suit a particular reader; and even where it is possible to provide a large staff of qualified and experienced librarians that would be needed to give personal attention to any considerable number of borrowers, few of the latter would secure the same satisfaction as they would from personal book selection and the danger of the staff, however unwittingly, imposing their own views upon readers would be present.

(b) Consequently only with open access can readers enjoy that full liberty of choice which is one of the library's primary duties to ensure.

(c) Very few people, before they become regular users of a library, know precisely what they want to read; very few know enough about books in general to use them fully and fruitfully. Only if they can wonder around the shelves, discovering something of the wealth and variety of the world of books, can the public library attempt its most important task - that of educating the public to make full use of books of permitting readers to discover and take advantage of the immense opportunities that exist for them today because most of what men have done, thought, dreamed and would achieve can be told on the printed page. The book is so important a factor in 20th century civilisation that unless people can read and have full free access to books they suffer an enslavement of mind, body and spirit which is totally inconsistent with democratic ways of life. Every library, even though it denies 'open access, is a weapon to dostroy their chains, but the library with closed access denies its users the fullest possible freedom.

Though these advantages - efficiency to the individual, freedom, enlightenment and education - are the paramount arguments for open access, we would mention others, in their own way, of considerable importance and economy.

(d) 'Closed' (i.e. non open access) libraries require more staff in relation to the amount of public use. In the closed library books have to be fetched by the staff; in open access libraries the readers 'fetch' their own books. And we have already noted that users of a closed library require considerable staff assistance whereas in open access library only a fent need to seek staff help. It is an undeniable fact that to issue say 100,000 books from a closed library, many more assistants must be employed than in an open access library issuing the same number.

(e) In actuality, however, no closed library issues as many books as does an open access library of comparable? size and book stock. As the overhead costs of these two libraries (rent, heating, lighting, cleaning, etc.) are probably much the same the actual cost per book borrowed must be much lower in the open access library.

(f) Moreover, the turnover of book stock in the closed library is much lower and there must be a serious tendency for those books which are best known to staff and readers to have a high turn over and those which are less known, to have a very low turnover, whereas in an open access library the demand is spread more evenly over the whole stock. This means that the average use of the stock is greater.

3. The Disadvantages of Open Access System. It cannot be denied that those who advocate the "closed" system may note certain, disadvantages of open access. Some - such as that with open access it is impossible to 'control' or 'dictate' the choice of readers -have no validity, for surely that is the last thing that a library today should want, or be able to do. That others are genuine will be agreed. For example.

(a) in an open access library the books are displaced, put out of order, made untidy; the books on the shelves must be put back into their proper places, by the staff, daily and weekly. But as this disorder and untidiness is a direct measure of the extent to which people have enjoyed their opportunity to study books it is surely a minor disadvantage. And, though the staff must spend a few hours daily on this task in the process they themselves learn much about books and so become better qualified to assist readers.

(b) The handling of books on the shelves by the public does involve some amount of wear and tear which does not arise in a closed library - but surely that handling has itself had some "educational" value.

(c) 'Open access' affords opportunities for the book thief. Undoubtedly, books are stolen from most open access libraries, and their librarians are concerned to reduce this loss. Nevertheless when losses through theft are balanced against the gains of open access they represent a running cost' which can reasonably be accepted. All shopkeepers suffer from thefts but the shopkeeper who kept his goods behind a counter and produced them only on request would soon go bankrupt.

4. Changing Over to Open Access

(a) The ideal open access lending library should be well lit, brightly decorated attractive, with bookshelves neither too low nor too high for convenience, with plenty of room between bookcases to enable readers to browse among the shelves in comfort, with occasional tables and chairs in which they can sit and sample books before they borrow them, with a desk for an assistant on duty to help borrowers to find what they want.

To achieve these conditions ample space is required. Librarians have been deterred from converting their libraries to open access because their libraries are not they may even be very difficult to make attractive, perhaps because they have little money and. fear that the conversion may be expensive.

These librarians are urged to believe that much more useful work can be done in the same space when the library is 'open access, even if it is not an ideal library, and that the process of conversion need not be expensive or difficult.

(b) The first step is usually to reduce the book stock. Most libraries (including many open access libraries) house too many books. In a closed library there are usually many items which, though they may be useful occasionally, are not likely to be wanted in demand often enough to justify their place in open access libraries. Those which are not useful at all should be discarded; for the remainder, rest storage space should be found either near the library or elsewhere. Remember that in an active library a considerable number of books are always in the hands of the readers. The books are returned and re-borrowed, and so on but no shelf space need to be provided for them; they are only 'temporary residents'.

(c) Secondly, remember that whereas the closed library usually has large counters and staff space, these are not necessary in an open access library. A simple small desk may well be sufficient, and if this can be put in an enteroom or corridor adjoining the room, so much the better.

(d) Don't put too many book cases into the new open access library. And remember that in an open access library *all* the books must be reasonably convenient to access. So either provide new cases no more than 6'6" high or out down the old ones.

(e) The books in an open access library *must* be classified though the classification need not be elaborate or over-detailed.

(f) Much can be done to prepare for the change-over while the library is still in use as a closed library. For example —

  (i) plan the layout of the open access library and so discover what shelf accommodation will be available.

  (ii) decide which books will be put on the open access shelves and which will be put into storage or discarded. Separate these categories. If the books for store can be taken there at once it may be possible to empty those bookcases which are to be used for the open access library and found them away to be out down in readiness.

  (iii) classify the open access stock, inserting the lables, etc. needed for open access 'charging' (the 'Brown' system is strongly advocated) and have the classification marks put on the books in readiness.

  (iv) prepare shelf and tier guides, etc.

  (v) prepare the new type of borrowers' tickets that will be needed.

  (vi) print a brief explanation of the new system for the information of readers.

(vii) if all these preparations are made, it will be necessary to suspend public service only so long as it takes to have the library redecorated, the lighting rearranged, the new shelving installed, etc.

(g) Instruct the staff of the new method. If possible, preferably well before anything is done towards conversion, send a senior assistant to work in a good open access library. He will learn much that will save time and money and ensure smooth working.

(h) Finally, realise that open access will be a new thing for most readers. Most of them, not used to finding their books for themselves, will feel lost at first. Arrange for them to have the maximum of help from the staff. Freedom takes some getting use to - but when its opportunities are appreciated the pleasure and the value of using the library will be, for all, immeasurably greater.

1.3.3.2. Closed Access Library

Closed Access Library is the library where users are not allowed to go near the documents directly. They first go to the library staff and asking for a document to read or lend, and then this staff will help the users to do so. In case of a big library having very less number of staff, this type of library system is very much useful. But from the users' view point it is not so useful so far as the information retrieval is concerned.

The advantages and disadvantages of 'Open Access Library System' will be the disadvantages and advantages of 'Closed Access Library System' respectively.

1.3.3.3. Partly Closed and Partly Open Access Library

In reality, most of the libraries are of neither 'Open Access' nor 'Closed Access' in nature. They have adopted partly open and partly closed access systems. In case of lending users are not allowed to go to the book shelves to choose their required documents, the stack rooms are closed for general users. But in many sections like Reading Rooms,

Reference, Periodicals, users can go to the shelves and can choose the documents for reading.

There are different kinds of libraries on the basis of different parameters, but the core objectives of each library is to collecting, organising, preserving and disseminating information and provide services to its users, to meet their demands.

REFERENCE

Almisned, Faisal Abdulaziz and ALanazi, Nasser ALhomide. (2007). Electronic Library System. Retrieved from *http://faculty.ksu.edu.sa/ykhlef/bahelorThesis/IS497Almisned.pdf*

Bhaurao, Telke Sudhakar. (2010). Recent trends in library and information science. *International Referred Research Journal,* 2(20). pp. 8-9

Bibliolatry. (2012). History of libraries. Retrieved from *http://bookworship.blogspot.in/2011/02/history-of-libraries.html*

Braude, R. M. (1995). The organisation of the digital library. *Academic medicine,* 70(4): 286–91.

Brophy, P. and S. Fisher. (1998). The hybrid library. New Review of Information and Library Research 4: pp. 3–15.

Casey, M. (2006). Born in the biblioblogosphere. *LibraryCrunch.* Retrieved from *http://www.librarycrunch.com/2006/01/post_1.html*

Casson, Lionel. (2001). Libraries in the ancient world. London: Yale University Press

Crawford, Walt. (2006). Library 2.0 and 'Library 2.0'. *Cites & Insights: Crawford at Large,* 6(2). Retrieved from *http://cites.boisestate.edu/civ6i2.pdf*

Deshpande, K. S. (1974). User Orientation in College Libraries. *Library Science with a slant to Documentation.* 15(12).

E-note. (2012). Library. Retrieved from *http://www.enotes.com/topic/Library*

Freidman, Thomas. (2006). The World is Flat. New York: Farrar, Straus and Giroux. Global Library Initiative. Retrieved from URL: http://www.globallibrary.org/en/index.php.

Gupta, Jyotsna. (2011). Types of libraries. Retrieved from *http://www.kuk.ac.in/userfiles/file/distance_education/Year-20112012/B_Lib%20lecture%201.pdf*

Halder, Sambhu Nath. (2009). Multimodal roles of library and information science professionals in present era. *International Journal of Library and Information Science (IJLIS).* 1(6). pp. 092-099. Retrieved from *http://www.academicjournals.org/ijlis*

Hutley, Sue, & Solomons, Terena. (2004). Generational change in Australian librarianship: viewpoints from Generation X. Presented at ALIA. Retrieved from http://www.library.uq.edu.au/papers/generational_change_in_australian_librarianship.pdf

IGNOU (1999a). Academic libraries: school, college and university libraries. BLIS Course material. Paper-I, unit-6, p. 29-47

IGNOU (1999b). Library development in modern India: Plans and programmes. BLIS Course material. Paper-I, unit-4 p. 45-57

IGNOU (1999c). National libraries, their function: A descriptive account of national libraries of India, UK and USA. BLIS Course material. Paper-I, unit-5, p. 5-25

IGNOU (1999d). Public libraries: role and functions. BLIS Course material. Paper-I, unit-7, p. 52-59

IGNOU (1999e). Special libraries and information centres. BLIS Course material. Paper-I, unit-8, p. 63-75

Jambhekar, Navin D. (2011). The traditional Library system and the framework to convert it into Digital Library: A case Study. *Indian streams research journal.* 1(6). Retrieved from *http://www.isrj.net/July/2011/Research_Paper_The_traditional_Library_system.html*

Jana, Sibsankar and Bhattacharya, Udayan . (2009). Towards Understanding Digital Objects. *IASLIC Bulletin.* 54(3).

Kipp, J. L., &. Kipp, C. R. (1961). Indian Libraries and the Indian Wheat Loan Educational exchange Program: A Report. New Delhi: The Wheat Loan Office, American Embassy p.78.

Kumar, Susheela. (1978). Physical Facilities in the Library. *Newfrontiers in Education.* 8, 27.

Lawson, S. (2006). Library 2.0: rapid response to rapid change. *Colorado Libraries,* 32 (2), 19-21.

Lenzini, Rebecca T. (2002). The graying of the library profession: a survey of our professional association and their responses. Searcher, 10(7). Retrieved from http://www.infotoday.com/searcher/jul02/refs

LIS 6010 Blog. (2009) Special Libraries. Retrieved from *http://lis6010blog.blogspot.in/2009/06/special-libraries-interesting-thing.html*

Maness, Jack M. (2006). Library 2.0 Theory: Web 2.0 and Its Implications for Libraries. Webology, 3(2).

McColvin, Lionel R. (1951). The open access library system. UNESCO-OAS Conference on the Development of Public Library Services in Latin America. Paris.

Metz, Terry. (2001). Wanted: library leaders for a discontinuous future. Library Issues, 21(3), 2-3.

Miller, P. (2006). Coming together around library 2.0: a focus for discussion and a call to arms. *D-Lib Magazine,* (12) 4, Retrieved from *http://www.dlib.org/dlib/april06/miller/04miller.html*

Ojha, D. G. (1980). University Libraries in India. Jodhpur: Latesh Prakashan, p.21.

Oppenheim, C. and Smithson, D. (1999). What is the hybrid library? *Journal of Information Science,* 25(2): 97–112.

Peek, R. (2005). Web publishing 2.0. *Information Today,* 22 (10), 17-18.

Pinfield, S. et. al. (1998). Realising the hybrid library. *DLib Magazine..* Retrieved from *http://mirrored.ukon.acuk/lis-journals/dlib/dlib/dlib/october98/10pinfield.html*

Rikowski, Ruth. (2005). Globalisation, Information and Libraries: The Implications of the World Trade Organisation's GATS and TRIPS Agreements. Oxford: Chandos Publishing.

Rosen, Robert, & Digh, Patricia. (2002). Developing Globally Literate Leaders. Retrieved from T+D, v55 n5 p70-75,78-81 May 2001. Record Details - EJ625924

Rowlands, I and Bawden, D. (1999). Digital Libraries: A Conceptual Framework. *Libri,* 49: pp. 192–202.

Rusbridge, C. (1998). Towards the hybrid library. *D-Lib Magazine.* Retrieved from *http://www.dlib.org/dlib/july98/rusbridge/07rusbridge.html*

Sharma, R. N. (1986). Indian Academic Libraries and S. R. Ranganathan: A Critical Study. Delhi: Sterling Publishers, p.95.

Sharma, P. L. (2005). Changing role of librarians in digital library era and need of professional skills, efficiency & competency. Retrieved from *https://drtc.isibang.ac.in/handle/1849/407*

Tebbutt, D. (2006). Is all the talk of web 2.0 just a lot of codswallop? *Information World Review,* (221), 9-9.

Wang, Xuemao, & Su, Chang. (2006). Develop Future Library Leaders with Global Literacy in the Context of Cultural Intelligence. *Chinese Librarianship: an International Electronic Journal,* 22. Retrieved from *http://www.white-clouds.com/iclc/cliej/cl22WangSu.htm*

Wikipedia, The free encyclopedia. (2012a). Library. Retrieved from *http://en.wikipedia.org/wiki/Library*

Wikipedia, The free encyclopedia. (2012b). Library. Retrieved from *http://en.wikipedia.org/wiki/Library#cite_note-4.*

Wikipedia, The free encyclopedia. (2012). Scriptorium. Retrieved from *http://en.wikipedia.org/wiki/Scriptorium*

WTEC Hyper-Librarian. (1999). Digital Vs traditional libraries. Retrieved from *http://www.wtec.org/loyola/digilibs/02_03.htm*

Yates, J. (1989). Control through communication. Baltimore, MD: Johns Hopkins University Press.

2

100 Years of LIS Education

Education, according to Radhakrishnan, is not a process of pumping information into empty containers. Education is a creative process moving from 'being' to 'becoming', from 'knowing' to 'internalising', from 'self-generated understanding' to 'a network of interactional activities leading on to 'gyaan'. To quote Radhakrishnan again, "All education is, on the one side, a search for truth; on the other side, it is a pursuit of social betterment."

Professional Education includes in its broadest outlines all that education, which has, direct value as preparation for professional calling or employment in life. It is differentiated on the one hand from the vocational education, which relates to those employment of social grade not recognized as professions and on the other hand from the general or so-called "liberal education" which has no specific practical application in view. The Librarianship has grown into full-fledged profession like law, medicine or accountancy. LIS education is treated as professional education. It includes all theoretical and practical education for collecting, processing, organizing and retrieval of right information to right people in right time through right way.

This is the centenary year of Library and Information Science (LIS) education in India. In the context of LIS education, Sarkhel (2006) highlighted that W. A. Borden, Librarian of Young Man's Institute; New Haven, Connecticut, USA started the first training program for library workers at Central Library in Baroda in 1911. In 1915, Asa Don Dickinson, another American Librarian, established a training course in erstwhile Punjab University (now in Pakistan), which is considered to be the second library school in the world, the first being the Columbia School. Both Borden and Dickinson who paved the way for LIS education in India were the students of Melvil Dewey. The outstanding contributions of Dr. S. R. Ranganathan gave a new impetus to the spread of LIS education at the university level in India. LIS education in India has expanded since independence in the form of increase in number of LIS departments in the universities and institutions offering specialized courses in LIS, and in the increase in number of students as well as courses. Dr. S. R. Ranganathan started a certificate course at Madras Library Association in 1929 which was taken over by the University of Madras, and in 1937 the course was converted into PGD in Library Science. This was the first diploma programme in Library Science in India. University of Delhi was the first university to run the full-fledged Department of Library Science in 1946 and started PG Diploma in 1947. Again in 1951 this diploma was changed to M.Lib.Sc.. Later between 1956-1959, six new LIS departments were started. After that a number of LIS department has continuously increased. Gradually M.Lib.Sc. has changed to MLIs i.e. Master of Library and Information Science. The computer courses was introduced in MLIS course in 1972. The M.Phil programme was started in 1978. The first Ph.D. was awarded to D.B.Krishna Rao in 1957 under the supervision of S.R.Ranganathan (Singh, 2003). Research has also been initiated and accelerated in different facets of the subject with the support of the universities and different funding agencies (Satija, 1993).

2.1. AIMS AND OBJECTIVES OF LIS EDUCATION

The aim of library and information science education is the preparation of LIS personnel for the task of successful performance at different levels of competence in different types of libraries and information centres with an insight into the role of these libraries and information centres in a fast changing society. It should impart a thorough grounding in the intellectual foundations of the profession and competence in the technical and technological skills required for their day-to-day practice in different positions. In other words, education for library and information science should be both knowledge and theory oriented task and practice oriented. The two aspects of theory and practice should blend harmoniously in a sound programme of library and information science education because on this will depend the effectiveness and success of the programme. In achieving this objective the methods of teaching and evaluation employed are as important as the quality of the faculty.

The main objectives of LIS profession are to: provide training for building up leadership qualities among the LIS profession; develop knowledge on the latest techniques of information storage, transfer and retrieval; help to acquire necessary skills in handling, accessing and application of electronic resources, tools and media; and help to know the latest developments in the Information Technology (IT)

LIS education has reached a juncture where its objectives need to be redefined. The basic aim behind LIS teaching should include the following objectives (Haridasan, 2003) also:

- To acquaint with the library activities
- To teach how to manage libraries using latest technology
- To make aware of responsibilities of libraries
- To make aware of their own responsibilities
- To help serve better, utilizing various services
- To teach about the professional ethics

The basic aims of library and information science education may be as follows:

- To develop administrative skills;
- To develop service orientation;
- To develop thorough knowledge of various sources of information, necessary to give the traditional and modern library services;
- To develop professional awareness.
- To develop necessary technical skills;

2.2. LEVELS OF LIS EDUCATION

The LIS education in India is offered at various levels such as certificate, diploma, degree, Associateship in Information Science (AIS), M.Phil and Ph.D. There are various universities and institutions worldwide offering LIS courses at different levels. Qualifications needed to pursue each course differ according to the level of the course and accrediting body. In the beginning the course was called as Librarianship, then Library Science and now it is called as Library and Information Science. So, universities provide degree i.e. Bachelor in Library and Information Science (BLIS); Masters in Library and Information Science (MLIS); M. Phil. in Library and Information Science and Ph.D. in Library and Information Science. But, some universities provide the degrees as Bachelor in Library Science (B. LIB); Master in Library Science (M.LIB), etc.

With the advancement of information and communication technology (ICT) and implementation of its advantages into the library management and services are the crucial part of the LIS profession. To cope up with the changing paradigm in LIS profession the curricula are being modified by the LIS schools. Some universities like Jadavpur University, Kolkata introduced 2-year Masters' degree in Library and Information Science (Digital Library). Besides these, National Institute of Science Communication and Information Resources (NISCAIR) under the Council of Scientific and Industrial Research (CSIR), New Delhi conducts a two-year programme leading to the award of Associateship in Information Science (AIS); the Documentations Research and Training Centre (DRTC) at the Indian

Statistical Institute, Bangalore offers the programme Associateship in Documentation and Information Science (ADIS) and these awards are also recognised as equivalent as to Masters in Library and Information Science (MLIS).

The courses in various levels, duration, pre-requisite qualifications to take admission and opportunities for job are summarized hereunder (Singh, 2003):

(a) **Certificate Course:** Many polytechnic colleges, schools and Library Associations impart the low level of library science courses in India having duration of few months to one year. However, some departments in universities and affiliated colleges are also conducting this course. The basic qualification for these courses is 10+2. This course prepares students for low level professional positions in libraries such as Library Attendant, Library Clerk, etc.

(b) **Undergraduate Diploma Course:** The Diploma courses are conducted at two levels, that is undergraduate and postgraduate levels. Undergraduate courses are conducted by women polytechnics as a two-year course after higher secondary or intermediate. It prepares students to be junior librarian and hold library assistant positions.

(c) **Postgraduate (PG) Diploma Course:** PG courses in some selected LIS areas of specialization are offered at the university level as a one-year course after the Bachelor of Library and Information Science programme. At present, only three universities and one deemed university are offering these programmes (Association of Indian Universities, 2003). They are a) University of Kerala, PG Diploma in Information Technology ; b) University of Mysore, Post MLIS Diploma in Library Automation; c) Gandhigram Rural Institute, PG Diploma in Archives & Documentation Management (UGC Model Curriculum, 2001, p.102); and d) University of Hyderabad, PG Diploma in Library Automation and Networking (Association of Indian Universities, 2003, p.2)

(d) **Bachelor of Library and Information Science (BLIS):** This is a one-year degree course conducted by universities after students graduate with a basic degree. However, in some colleges, Library Science is offered as an optional subject at the Bachelor of Arts level. For this, the students opt for Library Science as one of the optional paper, along with other optional papers in social sciences or the humanities. Students passing with this option would be considered at par with other degrees (UGC Model Curriculum Report, 2001, p.97). Bachelor's degree prepares students for professional positions in college and university libraries or as a school librarian. At present, 120 Indian universities are offering BLIS.

(e) **Master of Library and Information Science (MLIS):** Master of Library and Information Science is imparted as a one-year post graduate degree course in some universities while in some, it is conducted as a two year integrated course. It is a post-graduate course offered after BLIS. Presently, a total of 99 universities are offering MLIS, 21of them are offering two-year integrated course directly after BLIS. Many of the universities, which were initially offering BLIS and MLIS courses have now switched over to a two-year integrated course. The North East Hill University (NEHU) was the first Library and Information Science Education in India University to start the course in 1986, followed by the University of Madras in 1988. In 1989, Madras also started MLIS through distance education. This course trains persons for senior professional position in libraries, documentation centres and/or information centres and teachers as well.

(f) **Associateship in Information Science:** The National Institute of Science Communication and Information Resources (NISCAIR), New Delhi , formerly INSDOC also impart two years documentation programme i.e., Associateship in Documentation (AID) after graduation. The qualification for admission to the NISCAIR's programme is a master's degree in any subject or a BLibSc /BLIS with three years library experience. The Documentation Research and Training Centre (DRTC), established in 1962 in Bangalore, is also awarding ADIS. It offers two year Associateship in Documentation and Information Science (now known as Master of Science in Information Science). Admission requirement to DRTC is a Bachelor's degree in library science or a Master's degree in any subject with a minimum of two years library experience.

(g) **Advanced Training Course in Information Systems Management and Technology:** This one-year advanced training course in Information Systems Management and Technology is provided by the National Centre for Science Information (NCSI), an autonomous organisation under University Grants Commission (UGC) located at Indian Institute of Science (IISc), Bangalore. (Dutta and Das, 2001, p.25).

(h) **Other Specialised Programmes:** The Indian Association of Special Libraries and Information Centers (IASLIC) and the National Archives of India also offers specialised courses. IASLIC offers a one-year diploma programme in special librarianship and the National Archives of India offers a one-year diploma programme in archives and related subjects (Patel and Krishan Kumar, 2001, p.212).

(i) **M. Phil in Library & Information Science:** M. Phil. in Library and Information Science prepares a student for further advanced research in LIS. This is a research programme offered by university departments after one's completion of MLIS. As candidates having more qualifications are being preferred for superior position, many students are opting for M.Phil. Courses to better equip them for better positions. The University of Delhi started this programme in 1978, followed by many other universities such as Andhra, Tirupati, Annamalai, Vikram (Ujjain), and Gulbarga. At present there are 16 universities offering this programme. The basic requirement for admission is similar in all the universities but the duration of the course may vary.

(j) **Ph. D. Programme:** This is an advanced level research programme being offered after the completion of MLIS or M.Phil degree in library science. The general aim of a research degree, whether M.Phil. or Ph.D. is to provide training in doing research as well as to develop in the candidate a critical and analytical process of thinking with the purpose that they would be able to provide leadership in the profession. They would also be able to help librarians and information scientists to develop techniques and skills required to meet their requirements of the fast changing society. They should be able to identify the needs, set objectives, identify and analyze the problems and find appropriate solutions. They would also be in a position to participate in the planning, organization and implementation of programmes at various levels. Today, 64 universities in India are providing facilities for the Ph.D programme. The general qualification for admission is MLIS, but now the course work is compulsory for taking registration into Ph.D. programme.

(k) **D. Litt. Programme:** Two universities, i.e. Banaras Hindu University, Varanasi and Utkal University, Bhubaneswar offers D.Litt. programme in library science. So far only one D.Litt. degree had been awarded in India since 1992 by Utkal University, Bhubaneswar, to Dr D.B.Shukla on the topic 'The work and impact of a pioneer in library and information science: a critical study of the works of Prithvi Nath Kaula'(Kumar, 1998, p.8).

2.3 MODES OF LIS EDUCATION

Preparation for professional careers in librarianship entails education at the master's level in many parts of the world. In North America, a degree from a program accredited by the American Library Association (ALA) is the credential preferred by most employers. While the content of library/information science education still includes traditional subjects such as reference, collection development, cataloging, and management, programs are including more courses on technology and electronic resources. Many programmes are offering at least some of their courses online. Continuing learning is essential in order for librarians to adapt to rapidly changing information environments (Varlejs, 2010).

2.3.1. Direct Mode of LIS Education

There are number of university departments offering the LIS courses. This course is also available through distance learning mode. Two Sanskrit universities, viz., K S Darbhanga Sanskrit University (Bihar), and Sampuranand Sanskrit Vishvavidyalaya (Varanasi) offer Pustakalaya Vigyan Shastri (9 months) and Granthalaya Vigyan Shastri (One year) courses respectively. Knowledge of Sanskrit language is an essential requirement. LIS courses are available in the following Universities/Institutes:

Table 3. University Departments Offering Regular Courses (Singh, 2003)

No	*University*	*Dpt.Estd*	*BLIS*	*MLIS*	*M.Phil*	*Ph.D*
1	Aligarh Muslim University Aligarh	1958	1958	1971	—	1961
2	Amravati University, Amravati	1987		0	—	—
3	Andhra University, Vishakhapatnam	1935	1936 nc	1979; Intg 1994	1989	1980
4	Annamalai University, Annamalainagar	1979	1979	0	—	—
5	Babasaheb Bhimrao Ambedkar University, Lucknow	1997	—	MSc Into Sc. Intg	—	—
6	Banaras Hindu University, Varanasi	1942	1942	1965	—	1972
7	Bangalore University, Bangalore	1973	1973 nc 1975	Integ 1998	—	1981
8	Bharati Vidyapeeth,Pune	1997		—	—	—
9	Bhavnagar University, Bhavnagar	1982	1980	1991	—	—
10	Birla Institute of Technology, Ranchi	1993	—	M.Sc Info Sc Integ	—	—

No	*University*	*Dpt.Estd*	*BLIS*	*MLIS*	*M.Phil*	*Ph.D*
11	Bundelkhand University, Jhansi	1986	—	—	—	—
12	Burdwan University, Rajbati	1965	1965	1980	—	—
13	Calcutta University, Kolkata	1945	1945	1975	—	1972
14	Calicut University, Calicut	1975	1975	—	—	—
15	Delhi University, Delhi	1946	1947	1948	1978	1952
16	Documentation Research & Training Centre(DRTC, Banglore)	1962	—	1962 AIS 2 Yr	—	1962
17	Dr. Babasaheb Amebedkar Marathwada Univ, Aurangabad	1968	1968	1985		—
18	Dr. Bhim Rao Ambedkar University, Agra	1984	1984	1996	—	—
19	Dr. C V Raman University of Science, Technology, Commerce & Mgt, Raipur	2002	BLSIT	MLSIT	—	—
20	Dr. Harisingh Gour Vishwavidyalaya, Sagar	1970	1970	1983	—	
21	Gandhigram Rural Institute, Gandhigram (Deemed univ)	1990		—	—	—
22	Gauhati University, Gauhati	1966	1966 nc	Integ 1982	—	—
23	Gujarat University, Ahemdabad	1964	1964	1986	—	—
24	Gujarat Vidyapeeth, Ahemdabad	1986		—	—	
25	Gulbarga University, Gulbarga	1979	1979 nc	1985; Integ 1998	1987	1979
26	Guru Ghasidas University, Bilaspur	1988	1988	1995	—	—
27	Guru Nanak Dev University, Amritsar	1970	1973	1984	—	—
28	H N Bahuguna Garhwal University, Srinagar	1991	yes	yes	—	—

No	*University*	*Dpt.Estd*	*BLIS*	*MLIS*	*M.Phil*	*Ph.D*
29	Jadavpur University, Kolkata	1964	1965	—	—	—
30	Jamia Miha Islamia, New Delhi	1985	1987	—	—	—
31	Jammu University, Jammu	1971	1983	1985	—	1985
32	Jiwaji University, Gwalior	1984	1965	1984	—	1985
33	Kalyani University, Kalyani	1992	—	—	—	—
34	Karnatak University, Dharwad	1962	1962 nc	1971; Integ 1997	—	1974
35	Kashmir University, Srinagar	1970	n c	Integ	—	—
36	Kerala University, Thiruvananthpuram	1961	1961	1979 & PGDIT	—	1981
37	Kurukshetra University, Kurukshetra	1969	1965	1985	—	—
38	Kuvempu University, Shimonga	1993	—	MSc Integ 1993	—	1994
39	Lalit Narayan Mithila University, Darbhanga	na.	1976	—	—	—
40	Lucknow University, Lucknow	1971	1962	—	—	1984
41	Madras University, Chennai	1960	1936	1977; MSc Integ 1993	—	1977
42	Madurai Kamraj University, Madurai	1975	1974	1982		1982
43	M.S University of Baroda, Baroda	1956	1957	1986	—	—
44	Mahadev Desai Samajseva Mahavidyalaya	1986	—	—	—	
45	Mahatma Gandhi Gramodaya Vishwavidyala, Chitrakoot	1993	1993	yes	—	yes
46	Mahatma Gandhi Kashi Vidyapeeth Varanasi	1987	1983	—	—	—
47	Mahatma Gandhi University, Kottyam	n a	yes	—	—	—
48	Makhanlal Chaturvedi Rashtriya Patrakarita Vishwavidyalaya, Bhopal	1993	1993 Integ3yr	1994 Integ 2yr	—	—
49	Mangalore University, Mangalore	1982	1982nc	1990; Integ 1996	—	1991

No	*University*	*Dpt.Estd*	*BLIS*	*MLIS*	*M.Phil*	*Ph.D*
50	Manipur University, Imphal	1986	1986	—	—	1988
51	Mohanlal Sukhadia University, Udaipur Mother Teressa Womens' Univ.,	1975	1975	1995	—	yes
52	Kodaikanal	1999	—	M Sc Integ	—	
53	Mumbai University, Mumbai	1944	1944	1968	—	1971
54	Mysore University, Mysore	1965	1965nc	1971; Integ 1990	1994	1976
55	Nagarjun University, Guntur	1993	—	yes	—	—
56	Nagpur University, Nagpur National Institute of Science Comm	1956	1956	1984	—	1985
57	Info Resources (formerly Insdoc),	1952	—	1964 AIS 2 yr	—	—
58	North Bengal University, Siliguri	n a	yes	—	—	—
59	North Gujarat University, Patan	1992	1992	yes	—	—
60	North Maharashtra University, Jalgaon	2000	—	yes	—	—
61	North Orissa University, Takatpur	2001	yes	—	—	—
62	Osmania University, Hyderabad	1959	1959	1979	yes	yes
63	Punjab University, Chandigarh	1960	1960	1970		1972
64	Patna University, Patna	1980	1980	yes	—	—
65	Pt. Ravishankar Shukla University, Raipur	1971	1971	1987	nc	yes
66	Pune University, Pune	1958	1958	1979 now Integ.	yes	1981
67	Punjabi University, Patiala	1969	1969	yes		yes
68	Rabindra Bharati University, Kolkata	1985	1985	yes	—	yes
69	Rajasthan University, Jaipur	1960	1961	1974	—	1975
70	Rani Durgavati Vishwavidyalaya, Jabalpur	1998	—	yes	—	—
71	Sambalpur University, Sambalpur Sampurnanand Sanskrit Vishwavidyalaya,	1976	1976	1985	1994	1985

No	*University*	*Dpt.Estd*	*BLIS*	*MLIS*	*M.Phil*	*Ph.D*
72	Varanasi	1967	1967	—	—	—
73	Sardar Patel University, Vallabh Vidyanagar	1982	1982	1988	1991 nc	yes
74	Saurashtra University, Rajkot	1976	1976	1987	yes	—
75	Shivaji University, Kolhapur	1965	1965	hiteg		—
76	S.N.D.T. Women's University, Mumbai	1961	1961	1978	—	1985
77	South Gujarat University, Surat	1986	1986	2yrpt	—	
78	Sri Krishnadevaraya University, Anantpur	1982	1984nc	1990; Integ 1998	yes	yes
79	Sri Venkateswara University, Tirupati	1974	1974	1974; Integ 1984	yes	yes
80	Swami Ramanand Teerth Marathwada University, Nanded	1994	—	1994	—	1994
81	Swami Ramanand Teerth Marathwada University, Pune	na	yes	—	—	—
82	Tilak Manjhi Bhagalpur University, Bhagalpur	1971	1971	yes	—	yes
83	Utkal University, Bhubaneswar	1981	1982 nc	1984 Integ	—	1985
84	Vidyasagar University, Midnapore	1985	1985	yes	—	yes
85	Vikram University, Ujjain	1957	1957	1971	—	1976

Notes:

i. **Abbreviations Used:**

n a Not available

n c Now ceased

Integ Integrated two-year programme

— Part time

ii. **Symbols Used:**

— Course not being conducted.

— Course is being conducted but year of starting could not be found.

iii. The year of starting of the Dept/ Institution as well as the courses has been given wherever available.

Table 4. Colleges and Institutions Affiliated to Universities (Regular Courses)

No	*College/ Institute*	*Year*	*Affiliating University*	*BLIS*	*MLIS*
1	AEC Training College & Centre	1962	MG Gramodaya Vishwavidyalaya, Panchmarhi	-	
2	Arya Vidyapeeth Kanya Mahavidyalaya	na	University of Rajasthan, Bhusawar		-
3	Asian Workers Development Institute	na	Sambalpur University, Rourkela		-
4	Bishop Heber College, Tiruchirapalli	1983	Bharathidasan Univ, Coimbatore	-	Integ
5	Central Institute of Library Science	1970	Osmania University, Hyderabad		-
6	Dr Bhagwan Das Kendriya Granthalaya, Varanasi	1992	Mahatma Gandhi Kashi Vidyapeeth, Varanasi		_
7	Farook College, Calicut	na	Calicut University	—	-
8	Govt Girls Degree College	n a	Jiwaji University, Gwalior		
9	Govt MLB Arts & Commerce College, Lashkar	1962	Jiwaji University, Gwalior		
10	HPT Arts/ RYK Science College	1984	University of Pune, Nasik		
11	Institute of Correspondence Education	1981	University of Madras, Chennai		
12	Institute of Management Education	2002	CCS University, Ghaziabad, Meerut		-
13	International College of Girls	1962	University of Rajasthan, Jaipur		-
14	Isabella Thobum College	n a	University of Lucknow, Lucknow	-	-
15	JLNS College, Ganj Basoda	1998	Barkatullah University, Bhopal		
16	Jai Hind Defence College	1998	Barkatullah University, Bhopal		

No	*College/ Institute*	*Year*	*Affiliating University*	*BLIS*	*MLIS*
17	Kamta Prasad Guru Bhasha Bharati	1968	Rani Durgavati Vishwavidyalaya, Jabalpur		-
18	Mahendraguru Bhagwandas Granthalaya, Kashi Vidyalaya	na	Lucknow University, Lucknow		-
19	Majlis Ars & Science College, Valanchery	na	Calicut University, Calicut		-
20	Manair College of Library Science	1991	Kakatiya University, Khammam		-
21	Nehru Institute of Social Studies	na	Tilak Maharashtra Vidyapeeth, Pune		-
22	Nutan Maratha Mahavidyalaya	1992	North Maharashtra, Jalgaon		-
23	Onkannal Somani College of Commerce, Jodhpur	1987	Jai Narayan Vyas University, Jodhpur		-
24	Pt Nilakantha College of Library & Information Science.	n a	Utkal University, Bhubsneswar		
25	Rajeev Gandhi College, Bhopal	1997	Barkatullah University, Bhopal		
26	R K. Memorial Mahavidyalaya, Vidisha	1998	Barkatullah University, Bhopal		-
27	S.B Women's College, Cuttack	1973	Utkal University, Bhuhaneswar	-	Integ
28	SMIT College of Library & Information Science, Ankushpur	1983	Behrampur University, Behrampur		
29	Sant Sambhji Shinde College of Library Science, Parbhani	1995	Swami Ramanand Teerath Marathwad University	-	-
30	S S Patil Arts, T T Salunkhe Com & GR Pandit Science College, Jalgaon	n a	North Maharashtra, Jalgaon	-	
31	Vidya Bharti Science College	1987	Araravati University, Amravari		
32	Vikramaditya College	2000	Barkatullah University, Bhopal		-

(*Source*: Singh, 2003)

Notes:

i. **Abbreviations Used:**

n a	Not available
n c	Now ceased
Integ	Integrated two-year programme
—	Part time

ii. **Symbols Used:**

—	Course not being conducted.
—	Course is being conducted but year of started could not be found.

iii. The year of starting of the Dept/ Institution as well as the courses has been given wherever available.

Beyond the conventional regular courses of learning, Distance Learning System (DLS) assess to wide range of people who have some difficulties to attend classroom learning. Distance learning system gives wider access to higher education to persons of all ages and sex residing anywhere in the nation, especially to in-service persons, those could not undergo the higher education in regular conventional system for different reasons. It provides a system of student-centred self-paced learning, which provides opportunity to improvement of professional skills and competence of individuals who enjoy taking education as life-long learning. Finally it ensure, as far as feasible, appropriate value addition to career prospects in prevailing market opportunities.

2.3.2. Distance Mode of LIS Education

Distance education system could be defined in different ways. According to online dictionary of library and information science, distance learning is a method of instruction and learning designed to overcome barriers of time and space by allowing students to study in their own homes or at local facilities, often at their own convenience, using materials available electronically or by mail. Communication with the instructor is normally by telephone or e-mail. Telecommunication networks and teleconferencing have facilitated distance learning. Libraries are working to support distance learning by providing online catalogs and databases, electronic reserves, electronic reference service, online tutorials and electronic document delivery service (Reitz, 2004).

The United States Distance Learning Association defines it as "education program whereby students may complete all or part of an educational program in a geographical location apart from the institution hosting the program; the final award given is equivalent in standard and content to an award program completed on campus" (United States Distance Learning Association, USDLA). The history of distance education in Library and Information Science can be traced back as far as known to one year after Melvil Dewey opened the first formal programme of Library Science education in Columbia College. After all correspondence study was one of the first types of distance education employed in this field.

Open and distance education systems have started internet-based online methods, which offer more sophisticated online education, by using intelligent multimedia Online, internet-based access to web resources, computer-mediated communication using automated response systems and campus portal access to institutional processes and resources.

Salient Features of Distance Education

The system of classroom education that has been established for centuries has recently undergone great changes, many of which provoked by the growing demands of the population requiring increased culture and professional training but which for various reasons, like the distance, work and cost, etc. cannot attend traditional courses. New distance courses are offered somewhere frequently, but in general the public considers distance education as a second class or supplementary education at most. There are some points to highlight that the distance education system has acquired:

- Distance education is a predominantly learner-centred system that supports independent learning primarily based on course material in self-learning format.
- Teachers and students are separated by distance and time.

- Technology tools are used for communication, delivery, collaboration and cost containment.
- Opportunity for more students to receive quality education
- Flexible educational system that is not limited by age, time and place restrictions.
- It can supplement the studies of regular students along with being a separate system of education.
- This system facilitate learner to progress at his own speed.
- It is an ideal system to fulfill the need of those learner(s) who fall out of the conventional stream for different reasons.
- This system could reach any remote area through postal service if not through television.
- It leads to self-learning which is education in the real sense and stable and also which is not really encouraged in most of teaching institutions.

Evolution of Distance Education in India

As the formal system was unable to meet the demand for higher education in India, the planning commission in its third 5-year plan (1961-1966) recommended the introduction of Distance Education at the university level. The period 1962 to early 1980s was the correspondence education phase. The 1970s saw a spurt in the growth of correspondence education. The 1980s and 1990s are referred to as the open university phase. Indira Gandhi National Open University (IGNOU) was established by an Act of Parliament in 1985. Dr. B.R. Ambedkar Open University, Hyderabad (then known as Andhra Pradesh Open University) is the first open university in India offering Library and Information Science programmes through correspondence at Bachelor's Degree and Masters Degree from 1985 and 1998 respectively, followed by the University of Madras, Indira Gandhi National Open University (in 1989) started BLISc and later MLISc and Ph.D. programs. The growth of distance education programmes in India has created an outbreak in the library profession as unwanted quantitative expansion affected the professional caliber and the quality of education being imparted. The latter part of the 1990s saw the beginning of the virtual education phase when online courses were introduced by educational institutions.

Nowadays, the following LIS courses are offered by various open and distance education institutions in India:

- Certificate course in Library and Information Science (CLIS)
- Diploma in Library and Information Science (DLIS)
- B.Lib.Sc. /BLIS (Bachelor Degree in Library and Information Science)
- M.Lib.Sc. /MLIS (Master Degree in Library and Information Science)
- PGDLAN (Post-Graduate Diploma in Library Automation and Networking)
- M.Phil. (Master of Philosophy) in Library and Information Science
- Ph. D (Doctor of Philosophy) in Library and Information Science

A list of institutions offering various courses in Library and Information Science under distance mode in India is given in Table 5.

All Open/Distance Education Institution are arranged alphabetically under their concern state. Date of Gazette Notification regarding establishment of the universities is given within square brackets immediately after name of Open/Distance education institution. Yes or No indicates whether the institution offered the degree or not.

SWOT analysis of LIS Learning in Distance Mode

SWOT analysis is a tool that identifies the strengths, weaknesses, opportunities and threats of an organisation. The method of SWOT analysis is to take the information from an environmental analysis and separate it into internal (strengths and weaknesses) and external issues (opportunities and threats). Once SWOT is completed,

Table 5. Universities offering LIS courses through distance mode

S.N.	*State*	*Name of open/distance education institution*	*BLIS*	*MLIS*	*M.Phil.*	*Ph.D.*	*Others*
1.	Andhra Pradesh	Dr. B.R. Ambedkar Open University [1982]	Yes	Yes	No	No	No
2.	Andhra Pradesh	Kakatiya University [1976]	Yes	No	No	No	No
3.	Andhra Pradesh	Sri Venkateswara University [1954]	Yes	No	No	No	No
4.	Andhra Pradesh	Andhra University [1926]	No	Yes	No	No	No
5.	Bihar	Nalanda Open University [1995]	Yes	Yes	No	No	No
6.	Bihar	Lalit Narayan Mithila University [1972]	Yes	Yes	No	No	No
7.	Bihar	Patna University [1917]	Yes	No	No	No	No
8.	Haryana	Kurukshetra University [1956]	Yes	Yes	No	No	No
9.	Kerala	University of Calicut [1968]	Yes	No	No	No	No
10.	Madhya Pradesh	Awadesh Pratap Singh University [1968]	Yes	No	No	No	No
11.	Madhya Pradesh	Barkatullah University [1970]	Yes	Yes	No	No	No
12.	Madhya Pradesh	Dr. Hari Singh Gour Vishwavidyalaya [1946]	Yes	Yes	No	No	No
13.	Madhya Pradesh	Guru Ghasidas University [1983]	Yes	Yes	No	No	No
14.	Madhya Pradesh	Mahatma Gandhi Gramodaya Vishwavidyalaya [1991]	Yes	Yes	No	No	No
15.	Maharashtra	Yashwant Rao Chavan Maharashtra Open University [1990]	Yes	No	No	No	No
16.	New Delhi	Indira Gandhi National Open University [1985]	Yes	Yes	No	No	PGDLAN
17.	Rajasthan	Kota Open University [1987]	No	No	No	No	Diploma in LIS

S.N.	State	Name of open/distance education institution	BLIS	MLIS	M.Phil.	Ph.D.	Others
18.	Tamil Nadu	Vinayaka Missions University, Directorate of Distance Education [2005]	Yes	Yes	Yes	No	Certificate in LIS
19.	Tamil Nadu	Alagappa University [1985]	Yes	No	No	No	No
20.	Tamil Nadu	Annamalai University [1929]	Yes	Yes	No	No	No
21.	Tamil Nadu	Bharathidasan University [1982]	Yes	No	No	No	No
22.	Tamil Nadu	Madurai Kamraj University [1965]	Yes	Yes	No	No	No
23.	Tamil Nadu	Madras University [1857]	Yes	Yes	No	No	No
24.	Uttar Pradesh	U. P. Rajarshi Tandon Open University [2004]	Yes	No	No	No	No
25.	West Bengal	Netaji Subhas Open University [1997]	Yes	Yes	No	PhD	No
26.	West Bengal	University of Kalyani, Directorate of Open & Distance Learning [1960]	No	No	Yes	No	No

this determines what may aid the firm in achieving its objectives and what obstacles must be overcome or minimised to achieve the desired results. According to Wikipedia SWOT analysis is a strategic planning method used to evaluate the strengths, weaknesses, opportunities, and threats involved in a project or in a business venture. It involves specifying the objective of the business venture or project and identifying the internal and external factors that are favorable and unfavorable to achieving that objective. Deshpande and Ashtikar (2005) have done the SWOT analysis of distance education in general way. With the help of SWOT analysis the entire LIS education system in distance mode might be evaluated properly. Overview of strengths, weaknesses, opportunities, and threats of LIS education under distance mode is evaluated properly.

Strengths

Now a days, LIS education in distance mode is gradually becoming popular. This system opens the door for those learners who have difficulties to enter conventional education in LIS. In this regards the strengths side of the said system is highlighted here:

- Large number of youth population waiting for higher education.
- Low cost of the education within reach of rural people and in-service students. Expenditure on account of salaries is also less than the conventional system.
- As much as necessary of individual learning opportunities.
- Abundance of technology and cyber culture abundant.
- Library facilities are provided for distance learners. Provision for acquisition of books and journals (both print and digital) and educational CDs, VCDs and DVDs falling within purview of the subjects offered by the university under distance mode are made.
- There is no restriction of physical boundary, so any eligible person from anywhere can pursue the required course.
- With the help of internet more programmes become effective

(online communication and feedback) and systematic where anybody could be able to reach host website from remote place within least possible time.

- Programmes are recognized by national level apex body like the University Grants Commission (UGC) and the All India Council for Technical Education (AICTE) and hence no fear of non-acceptability.
- It is more economical as compared with the conventional programmes for students as well as for organisation.
- More matured students, even some of them are employed in government or non-government institution. So, practical experience can help them to catch the knowledge in the concerned field.
- Useful interaction with the industries or world of work through employed students.
- No need to establish their own laboratory and appoint the teaching faculty members for practical classes.

Besides these, The Department of Education, Ministry of Human Resources Development, Government of India notified vide the Notification No. 44 dtd. 01-03-1995 published on Saturday, 8 April, 1995 in the Gazette of India that "*on the recommendation of the Board of Assessment for Educational Qualification, the Government of India has decided that all the qualifications awarded through Distance Education by the Universities established by an Act of Parliament or State Legislature, Institutions Deemed to be Universities under Section 3 of the UGC Act, 1956 and Institutions of National Importance declared under an Act of Parliament stand automatically recognized for the purpose of employment to posts and services under the Central Government, provided it has been approved by Distance Education Council.*" With all advantages discussed above, distance education system has established the field where increasing numbers of candidates enrolled every year.

Weaknesses

The ultimate aim of any professional course like LIS is to make job seekers enrolled in the system employable and marketable. The universities that have correspondence courses in LIS are not producing such candidates who have the adequate required skills. A close examination of the past studies (Mangla, 1998; Singh, 2003) reveals that there are lots of problems that confront the LIS education in India. A Brief description of the weakness wings of LIS education in distance mode are enlightened below:

Investment by Distance Education Centres

Finance is a major issue. Without appropriate financial support it is not possible to make any resource available. The agencies issuing grants like the UGC, university authorities and other bodies do not support LIS schools needing special grants for infrastructure, faculty and other necessary items.

Practical and Real-Field Hands-on-Experiences

Because of professional education LIS needs some practical and real-field hands-on-experiences to fit for different types of work environment. Most of the distance education study centers are conducting LIS education, which are not acquired well furnished computer laboratory and library facilities, communication equipments and other information science components that are required for LIS departments.

One of the main constraints of e-learning systems is that students need to know how to use the particular information technology. Much more attention will be required in the future web based training that will be delivered over the internet using the non propriety www server and client technology. Despite the increase in the number of institutions offering distance programmes, little is known about the teaching practices that contribute to effective online course design and delivery.

Teacher-Student Interaction

Being a practical oriented course, LIS education required computer training and practical classes for classification and cataloguing with personal contact between teacher and student, but the number of days for contact classes is very limited. Some universities are not even insisting that students attend contact classes. There is no provision of credit hours for individual papers in the distance programme.

Adequate Infrastructure

Space is one of the important requirements to create sound learning environment. Library facility is also a vital organ of any educational system. In distance education system all these factors are not always maintained properly. Besides this, it lacks full time faculty members and their teaching aids also.

Uniformity

There are no standard rules and regulations in the national level regarding selection criteria for admission, intake, class periods, teaching methodology, distribution of marks, methods of evaluation and research programmes in distance education system. So, it lacks uniformity.

Curricula and duration of LIS courses

Curricula of BLISc and MLISc are not uniform in library and information science schools; very little emphasis is given to the components that the LIS professionals need to carry out on the tasks in the library when they join the given job. However, one of the problems with e-learning in India is the lack of course content, especially outside the mainstream focus areas of IT education, English-language content and tutorial-like courses. There will be a high demand for people who can develop multilingual courseware that addresses various topics. The course duration at each level is also not uniform in the LIS schools. The correspondence courses had made their own style of nomenclature, curricula and duration. Most of the LIS schools have Masters Level of one-year/two semesters. Only one-year duration is not enough for a student to learn all the things at an advanced level.

Beyond the above mentioned weakness there are inadequate

training facilities to update the professional competence of in-service teachers. Existing UGC refresher courses failed to provide needed expertise and skills to meet the growing complexities of information environment and lack of internal quality assurance and accreditation mechanism (Singh, Shahid, 2010). In the true sense, the weakness may be turned into opportunities by the careful consideration of the said points.

Opportunities

Distance education is nothing but the process of acquiring knowledge and qualification without attending classroom on regular basis rather those who could not afford normal education due to some difficulties like non-availability of admission, finance, geographical location, suitable time, etc. Sacchanand (1998) opines some opportunities associated with LIS education in distance mode. Significant opportunities are summarised as below:

- It provides opportunities to acquire or update skills and knowledge in areas increasingly in demand.
- It enhances the already acquired professional qualification. Individual subjects may be taken as continuing education courses, without the need to meet formal entry requirements.
- It increases access to education and meets the needs of learners who are already in the workforce.
- It emphasises freedom from classroom limitations in location and time. Distance education is flexible with variable times and locations, whether at work or at home. Time to learn is expanded to fit individual needs.
- It offers a chance to information professionals and people who live and work in remote areas and have no way of improving and continuing their education.
- It creates opportunities for people with families and work commitments those are unable to further their studies at conventional universities.

- Opportunity to enroll youth who are not absorbed in conventional education system of Library and Information Science.
- Government support schemes are also available and hence possibility of getting adequate funds is there.
- Several new curriculum on the backdrop of globalization.
- Due to development of information and communication technology (ICT) and application of multimedia approach made the open and distance education more effective in term of curriculum delivery, contact lectures, audio-visual conferencing, etc. So, it is a good opportunities to up-gradation of skills and qualifications.
- Distance education system is highly accessibile worldwide. As there are no geographical boundaries, any remote learner can get access.
- Learners will be able to acquire project organisation image through virtual tools.
- More demand in future from the employed and remote learner.
- Need based or tailor made programme launching creates a good opportunity to new generation people.

In a single word, distance education system opens the door for all deserved people to higher learning and grows updated knowledge on their field.

Threats

Besides the opportunities associated with LIS education in distance mode there are some threats to enroll this system. The major threats are listed here:

- Authenticity of practical skills development may be questioned although in-service learners have good practical exposure; else some of the fresher face the lacuna of hands-on practice and to be fit for real field scenarios.
- Technical and vocational product of distance mode may get less preference than contact mode product.

- Open and distance universities affiliated by the apex body like the UGC and the AICTE and recognised by the Distance Education Council (DEC), Govt. of India, the regulatory apex body of ODL in India but, there is no over all acceptances by the industry and the world of work.
- Students in university-established area hesitate to register the programme with distance education.
- Need of getting programme accredited with apex educational or professional bodies like, the National Assessment and Accreditation Council (NAAC), National Board of Accreditation (NBA).
- The UGC berried to pursuing research programmes, like M. Phil. and/or Ph.D. from distance mode from the year 2009.
- While imparting practical skills, development component system will face lot of odds.
- Establishment of non-granted LIS schools here and there as mushroom.
- Large number of dropouts is another threat of this system. All though a pretty good numbers of students enrolled every year, but they are not completed their course in time.

The threats are to be converted into opportunities by entering into the collaborative distance education programmes with such institutes.

To cope with the changing paradigm, LIS professionals have to possess required knowledge and skill to apply it in real-field situation. Different kinds of libraries in the present era and job market expectations demands modernization of the teaching and learning pattern of library and information science education. Overall uniformity and quality maintain in LIS education is very much necessary without consideration of formal or informal mode of education. A coming into being of distance education system and its rapid spread in India and abroad has been possible due to advancement in information and communication technology (ICT). More and more people are now turning to the mode of distance education for widening their knowledge base and for becoming proficient in their work life. Therefore, now there is a need for devising a new online system that would act as a facilitator for the distance learners and help them in acquiring timely and relevant qualification. In this regard organized and focused efforts are needed by various agencies, viz., the Central Government, the State Government, the UGC, the AIU, University Administration, LIS professionals, teachers and students also. The curriculum of LIS education in India definitely needs to be based on the traditional library practices as well as modern trends for library functioning and services by adapting the ICT application. All stakeholders should be aware that the changing paradigm of LIS profession to cope with the challenges in the present era.

2.4. ROLE OF LANGUAGE IN LIS EDUCATION SYSTEM

Language is central to the whole process of education and is the principal means of cultural transmission. "Effective use of language," says Radhakrishnan, "is a powerful help to good scientific thinking and especially to communication in science, as well as a necessity in the humanities." No education, Tagore felt could be said to be creative unless it was given in his or her mother tongue. "Learning should as far as possible follow the process of eating. When the taste begins from the first bite, the stomach is awakened to its function before it is loaded, so that its digestive juices get fully play. Nothing like this, happens, however when the Bengali student is taught in English. When one is choking and spluttering over the spelling and grammar, the inside remains starved, and when at length the taste is felt, the appetite is vanished". English can be and should be used as a second window on the expanding universe around them. In a multilingual setting, the mother tongue should come first and then the other tongue in terms of their roles and functions.

This is what Tagore advocated firmly all his life. His writings present the vision of India.

" Where the mind is without fear and the head is held high;

Where knowledge is free;............

....

Where words come out from the
depth of truth;"..........

(*From Gitanjali, poem no. xxxv*)

The National Policy on Education was published by the Ministry of Human Resource Development, Govt. of India in 1986. According to this document, the new policy emphasizes the adoption of regional language as the media of instruction at the university stage.

System is a set of components, which interacts with each other to accomplish an objective. A system has its inputs, throughputs and outputs. The components of the system are called sub-system. The interconnections and interactions between sub-systems are termed as interfaces. Organizations are open systems, since they receive unplanned and unscheduled inputs from their environments and interact continuously with the environment and adapt in such a way as to continue their existence.

LIS education in an institute behaves like a system (Jana, 2006) (Fig. 5). This system is comprised of four interacting components/ sub-systems having a common goal i.e. to produce well-trained library personnel. Actually LIS education is an open system comprising of inputs, throughputs and outputs. Again it is interacting to its environments to keep the system alive/open. The elements of this system are enumerated as follows:

(a) Input : The inputs in this system are-

(i) Documents acquiring in the library on the umbral and penumbral subjects of LIS

(ii) Information acquiring by the teacher through refresher courses, Internet, online and by reading journal articles etc.

(iii) Teachers appointed

(iv) Research scholars registered

(v) Students admitted

(vi) Curriculum change

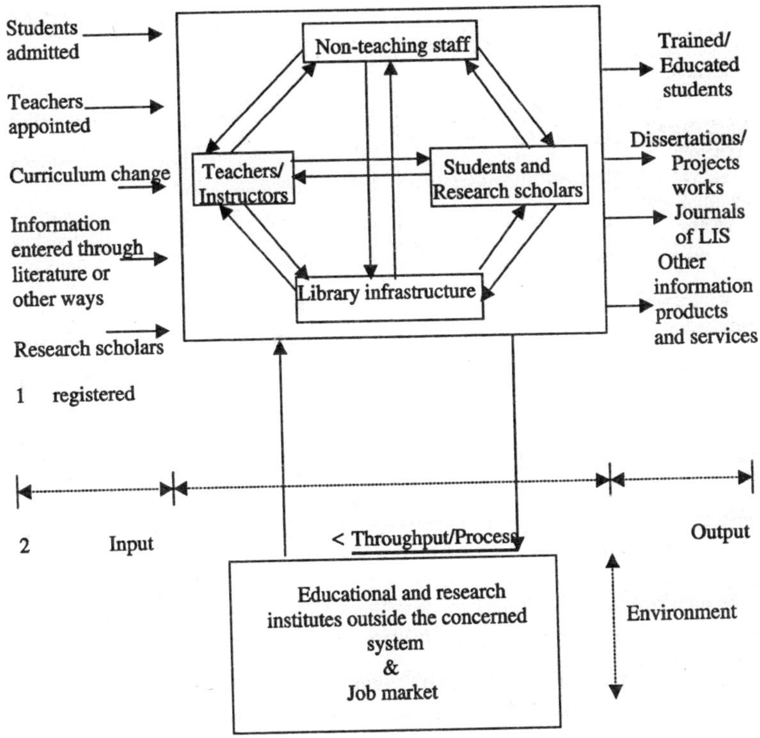

Fig. 5. LIS Education System

(b) **Throughput/process** : It consists of four interacting components. These are-

(i) **Teacher/Instructor** : Teaching faculty act as communicator/ receiver in information communication process. They convey their knowledge through classroom teaching and guided work to the students.

(ii) **Students and Research Scholars** : They come from different subject background and from different medium of education system. They act as receiver/communicator in information communication process.

(iii) **Library Infrastructure** : This component includes document on LIS, course materials, schedules, catalogue codes, indexing manuals, computer program software, Internet, online databases, educational aids, reprographic facilities and other library services. It also includes librarian.

(iv) **Non-Teaching Staff** : They are designated as peon, clerk, and library attendant. They ultimately coordinate the other three components by providing documents to teacher, students and research scholars, doing clerical works for conducting admission, classes and examinations.

(c) **Output** : Through the interactions of these four components, ultimate output comes out. The outputs are enlisted hereunder:

(i) Educated/trained LIS personnel
(ii) Dissertation papers
(iii) Project papers
(iv) PhD theses
(v) Journal articles
(vi) Other information products and services

(d) **Environment** : As this system is an open system, hence environment plays an important role. Here environment covers total society. But keeping conformable relation to the present study I consider two immediate environments viz. educational and research institutes of LIS outside the concerned system and job markets.

If we analyze the interfaces, teachers-students; environment-system; library-teachers, students and research scholars, then we can easily establish our scientific opinion regarding the suitable medium of instruction in LIS education. Let us go through analyses.

(i) **Teachers-Students interface** : Interaction between teachers and students are well represented by information communication process. In classroom teaching, teachers (communicator) provide message (LIS subject matter) through channel (language and medium) to the students (receiver). If students give feedback to the teachers after receiving message, then communication will be effective (Fig. 6).

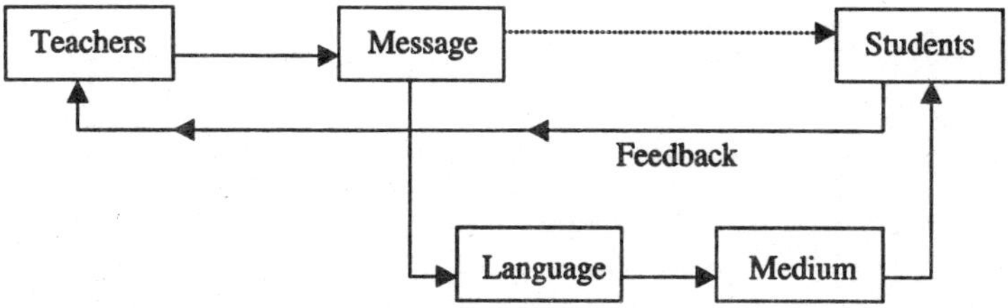

Fig. 6. Information communication process in classroom teaching

In this communication process language plays a vital role to encode the message. Again this language may act as a communication barrier, when it is not understandable to the receiver. Therefore they do not provide feedback. So students' existing knowledge structures are not modified and hence no absorption of information i.e. no feedback will take place. It is well expressed by the fundamental equation of information science given by Brookes.

$$K(S) + \Delta I = K(S + \Delta S)$$

Where, K(S) is the existing knowledge structure

$K(S+\Delta S)$ is the modified knowledge structure caused by absorption of information (ΔI)

ΔI is amount of information

It is proved through practice that feedback is greater if language is receivers' mother tongue. Again during examination/evaluation, students act as communicator. They communicate through written message or viva voce to the teacher (receiver). Actually these answers are the ultimate feedback of the students to the information/knowledge conveyed by the teachers during classroom teaching and guided works. After receiving answers (message), teachers give their feedback through providing marks/grade/class (Fig. 7).

Again during research, teachers communicate to research scholars through guided works. In this information communication process, the effectiveness depends on the language (i.e. medium of instruction).

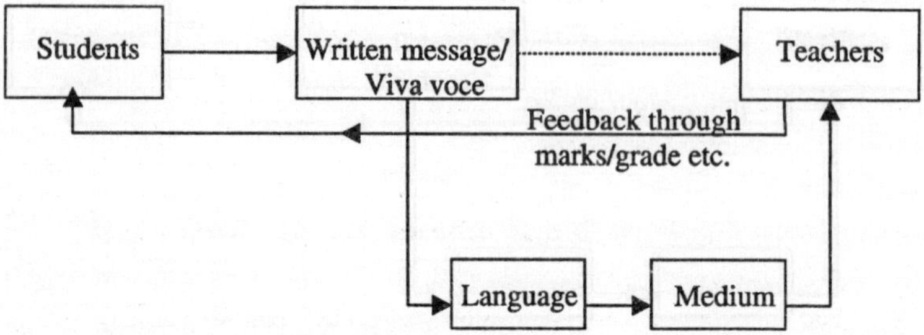

Fig. 7. Information communication process in examination/evaluation

(ii) **Library-Teachers, Students and Research scholars interface:** Keeping consistency to class lectures and class notes, sufficient amounts of documents in regional language are necessary in the library for free flow of information from documents to students and teachers. Computer software in regional language is very much needed in this regard.

(iii) **Environment-system interaction :** Two environments in the present study, by supplying inputs to the system and absorbing outputs from the system, keep the system functioning. The interactions with system are analyzed as follows-

(a) *Relation to other educational and research institutes* : If the medium of instruction is regional language, then it will be very tough job to communicate with the educational and research institutes of LIS whose medium of instruction is different. So there is little chance of isolation from the rest. Regarding research works, any institution should maintain relation to the educational and research institutes outside the concerned system.

(b) *Relation to Job market* : Job market plays an important role in education in general and in professional education in particular. Job market in India still provides opportunities to the LIS passed students those who have English as a medium of instruction. Interviews and examinations are conducted in English. Various newly emerging corporate sectors appoint Information officers those who are well sound in English. So LIS students educated through English get job easily than others.

If we provide education through regional language, then the immediate objective of education i.e. to create well knowledgeable/ well trained LIS personnel is fulfilled. But the ultimate objective of professional education i.e. to use theoretical knowledge in practice for the betterment of society is hampered, because most of the students educated through regional language may not get jobs.

But in reality, the scenario is not so, it is completely different. Actually there are different job markets for the LIS students of different educational levels.

In India, mainly three types of LIS education are in vogue, viz. Cert. Lib. Sc., BLIS and MLIS. regular or distance M. Phil. and Ph. D. programs in LIS are also conducted. In each level the environment of the system is different.

Table 6. The different levels and respective job markets

Level of Course in LIS	*Job Market*
Cert. Lib. Sc.	Librarian of Rural Library / Primary unit Libraries, etc.
BLIS	School Librarian; Asst. Librarian - Gr.II, in University Libraries; Librarian in Town Libraries, etc.
MLIS or Equivalent	University Asst. Librarian, College Librarian, Asst. Professor of LIS, etc.
M Phil or Ph. D.	Same as MLIS & promotion to higher scale.

In cases of Cert. Lib. Sc. and BLIS, the students after completion of courses, generally get employment in their respective states. So, regional language as a medium of instruction is not creating any problem in these two levels. Again most of the MLIS passed students and higher degree holders (M. Phil, Ph. D. etc.) generally get job in their respective states. Only few students find job in other states and in corporate sectors within the states, need sound English knowledge to collect, organize and disseminate information. Therefore, for the sake of majority of MLIS students, medium of instruction should be regional language.

Some problematic areas with respect to language and probable remedies:

From the above discussion it is clear that, regional language, as a medium of instruction will not create serious problem to provide education. But still we have to take several steps to build healthy environment for the same. The problematic areas and the ways to overcome these situations are as follows (Jana, 2006).

(i) Lack of standard terminology : In existing situation, standard terminology of LIS subject in regional language is very poor. New terminologies all over the world are emerging constantly in English language. As our regional languages are very rich in semantic value, so it is not a tough job for us to construct standard terminologies in these languages. In this respect we can organize seminar, symposium where experts on linguistics of English and of that particular regional language and LIS subject experts take part. Terminology must be from commonly usable words/phrases. In some cases, where no standard terms are being constructed in regional language, hypothecated words/phrases should be avoided and transliteration of English terms is adopted.

(ii) Scarcity of literature : There is real scarcity of textbooks and journals in regional languages. It is a big problem. Efforts should be taken to write and publish up-to-date LIS literature in regional languages as early as possible. Primarily, the LIS personnel should translate the existing Standard English works on LIS in the regional languages.

(iii) Availability of expertise : Teaching faculty has been mostly educated through English. So they feel comfortable to impart education in English. But they can easily switchover to regional language if it is their mother tongue. Again any expertise can join in any linguistic provinces of India, may face problem to teach in regional language of that particular area which is simply unknown to him/her. But it is very rare in practical situation in India. If it is so, teachers are advised to learn the language of the land after joining there. As all languages of India are of same origin, hence these are some how related to each other.

(iv) Attitudinal change of teacher : Initially teachers may find some difficulties to change their attitudes to teach in regional language, but once the change is introduced they will accept the change.

(v) Job market : Already discussed earlier that job market for Cert.Lib.Sc., BLIS students, are not squeezed out. But for MLIS/M Phil/Ph D passed students, the movement will be restricted. Again, it is a fact that this restriction is only for few students. Therefore these students are advised to learn English so that they can easily communicate in other settings where English is a must.

(vi) Background of students : The students from other medium of instruction feel uncomfortable to learn in regional language. In this situation teachers are expected to impart education in the regional language and in English side by side as much as possible. If possible, teachers may provide help to the students of other medium after classroom teaching.

(vii) Problems in All India basis competitive examinations : For all India basis examinations like NET, where there is no such choice of regional language to write answers except Hindi, students, other than English or Hindi medium may feel difficult. It is a real problem in any polyglot country like India. There is no such immediate way to overcome this critical problem. But if the government would take any decision to give permission to answer in recognized regional languages, stated in constitution of India, then the problem may be minimized.

From the above discussion, it is found that use of regional language, as a medium of instruction in different levels of LIS education in India will be effective and is also possible. But it is also fact that there is no such alternative for English in higher studies or research works to date. So, first, we have to do basement works for implementation of regional language as a medium of instruction. Then we can go for teaching-learning through regional language. Again also some acute problems will arise in providing teaching through regional language. We cannot and should not avoid global village concept in this information age. In the global perspective English is the international medium of communication. Therefore, besides education through regional language, English terminologies during classroom teaching should be used so that students can be well acquainted with the new emerging terminologies. Once they memorizes English terminologies they do not face big problem to speak and write LIS subject matters in English. Because, in India, students are from the very beginning acquainted with English as second language. Side by side there should be provision for students to complete project papers and colloquiums in English in each paper. It will help them to communicate through English during higher studies. In this respect, teachers can create and accelerate the students' appetite by giving references of English articles and other documents during classroom teaching so that they can consult the same. English language acts as a national as well as an international link language. In the very concluding sentence, regional language may be as the medium of instruction in LIS education in India, but also recommend English as the link language to keep pace with global advancement of the subject.

2.5. CURRICULUM DEVELOPMENT AND LIS EDUCATION IN INDIA

LIS curriculum change has been an inevitable continuous phenomenon in India. At the university level, the UGC mainly controls the general course structure of curricula. Since its inception, UGC has given due emphasis to curriculum design for LIS departments, along with developments in university and college libraries. The UGC being the single-most important statutory, advisory and Executive body, deliberately established to assist the Government in discharging its constitutional responsibility, has played an important role in the improvement of university libraries. Education has been a major concern of the Government which has since independence appointed various commissions and committees to make recommendations for the reorganisation of the Indian Education

System. The major library related commissions and committees appointed by the UGC are:

- The Library Committee (1957)
- Review Committee on Library Science (1961)
- The Education Commission (1964-66)
- Ranganathan Committee on Library Science in Indian Universities (1965)
- Mehrotra Committee (1983)
- Committee on National Network System for Universities/ Libraries (INFLIBNET) (1988)
- Curriculum Development Committee on Library and Information Science (1990-93)
- Rastogi Committee (1997- 1998)
- Karisiddappa Committee on Curriculum Development in Library and Information Science (2001)

2.5.1. The Library Committee (1957)

After the establishment of the UGC by the Act of Parliament in 1956, Dr. C.D. Deshmukh, its first Chairman, while drawing an analogy between a university and the human body, remarked that the students form the body of the university, the administration is the head, the teachers are the soul and the library is the heart. The UGC took effective measures by initially giving liberal grant of Rs. 1,00,000 for college and university libraries. Its aim was to develop institutions of higher learning and to strengthen library facilities in universities. One of the first acts of the UGC in this regard was to appoint the Library Committee in 1957 under the Chairmanship of Dr.S.R.Ranganathan. Other members of the Committee were Professor S.Bashiruddin, K.S.Hingwe, B.S.Keshavan and S.Parthasarathy. It is popularly known as 'Ranganathan Committee'. It was for the first time that the Government of India had sought advice from professional librarians. The Committee systematically surveyed the academic libraries and was very much disappointed to find poor facilities, services and budget of the university libraries. The Library Committee conducted a seminar on "Work Flow in University and College Libraries" at Delhi from March 4-7,1959 to apprise the librarians about the findings of their survey. The Committee submitted its report in 1959 making concrete recommendations on several aspects viz. library grant, purchase of books, cultivating reading habits, facilities for inter-library loan, photocopying, reference and documentation services, building a microfilm collection, open access system, preparation of union catalogue of books and serials to facilitate co-operation among libraries, library personnel library building and furniture.

A special grant should be provided to start library of the new university or a new department in the existing university. The formula should be revised from time to time to cover the inflation or any other unpredictable factor. The Library Committee also suggested appointing another committee to look into the standards of teaching, examination and research in library schools. A university should appoint full-time library science faculty for teaching rather than utilising merely the part-time service of the librarian(s). The librarians should possess prescribed professional qualifications. The Committee further observed that the status and the salary of the library staff should be same as that of the teaching and research staff. The UGC accepted the above stated recommendations of the Library Committee as norms for promoting university libraries. The acceptance of the recommendations cleared the obstacles and paved the way for library development. Some academic institutions successfully implemented these recommendations, but others could not adopt them. Since education was the responsibility of State Governments, they did not consider it binding for themselves to implement the recommendations of the UGC Library Committee (1957).

2.5.2. Review Committee on Library Science (1961)

In I960, very few universities were conducting certificate, diploma and degree courses in Library Science. There was neither any uniformity in admission rules and qualification criteria nor in curriculum or syllabus, practical training or quality of teaching. There were not many qualified professors of Library Science in the country. Therefore, librarians used to work as part-time faculty in library schools. Thus, the standard of both teaching and library work used to suffer. On the recommendation of the UGC Library Committee of 1957, a Review Committee on Library Science was appointed in 1961 under the Chairmanship of Dr. S. R. Ranganathan. Other members of the Committee were Dr. C. P. Shukla, K. A. Isaac, S. Bashiruddin, P. N. Kaula, B. S. Keshavan, Dr. J. S. Sharma and Professor S. Das Gupta, with Dr. P. J. Philip as the Secretary.

The responsibilities of the Review Committee were to recommend standards for teaching, examination and research in library schools. It had to prepare the curriculum for various level courses of Library and Information Science and decide the entrance qualification of the students for each course. The Committee had to suggest guidelines for conducting examinations and lay down minimum standards for passing them. The Committee submitted its report to the UGC in 1962. It:

- described the objective of library education;
- directed not to conduct Certificate level courses at the University;
- prepared curriculum outlines for Bachelor's and Master's degree courses;
- suggested pre-admission apprenticeship for six months in recognized library; and
- recommended staff-student ratio of 1:10 at the undergraduate level and 1:5 at the Master's level.

The Committee strongly recommended having close cooperation between the library and the department of Library Science of a university. It emphasised that Library Science faculty should work in the library for short periods and librarians should maintain academic interest and deliver a few lectures for the courses. But, the Committee disapproved employing library staff as part-time teachers in the library school instead of appointing full-time teachers. It was also emphasised that teachers of Library Science should be treated at par with the teachers of other departments in all academic and administrative matters of university. The UGC accepted all the recommendations of Review Committee for implementation by the library schools. The report of the Review Committee on Library Science entitled "Library Science in Indian Universities" was published by UGC in 1965.

2.5.3. Education Commission (1964-66)

In spite of the liberal grants given to the universities by UGC for the development of libraries, following the recommendations of Radhakrishnan Commission, the condition of the university libraries was far from satisfactory. The universities did not allocate enough funds for the development of their libraries and library services. In July 1964, the Government of India appointed Education Commission under the Chairmanship of Prof.D.S.Kothari to evaluate the education system as well as the libraries. This Commission is known as Kothari Commission (1964-66). The Commission stated in the final report— "Nothing can be more damaging than to ignore its library and to give a low priority. No new college, university or department should be opened unless adequate number of books are provided in the library." It also observed that with the increasing enrolment of students at the colleges and universities, the demand for the library services has been growing constantly. The library staffs have to cater to the diverse needs of the undergraduate and postgraduate students, research scholars and faculty members. The Commission felt the need for providing documentation services, especially indexing and abstracting, to satisfy research demands and help the university teachers in keeping abreast of new developments in their fields. The Commission laid emphasis on self study at the libraries and supplement lectures by tutorial instruction, easy accessibility of books, extending working hours and days, multiple copies of textbooks, separate sections for periodicals, reference books and research work so as to encourage students to visit the library, develop reading skills and raise the standard of library services. While commending the Radhakrishnan Commission for recommending either 6.25% of the total education budget of the university and college or Rs. 40.00 per student as annual grant for the library, the Kothari Commission also suggested monetary guidelines. "As a norm, a university should spend each year about Rs. 25.00 for each student and Rs.300.00 per teacher or from 6.5% to 10% of the total budget depending on the stage of development of each university library." The Commission remarked that the UGC should separately allocate foreign exchange for the academic libraries. The academic librarians, however, were not very happy with the recommendations of Kothari Commission. They felt that more reasonable figure per student and teacher should have been arrived at rather than lessening it from Rs 40.00 per student recommended by the Radhakrishnan Commission to Rs. 25.00 per student considering the increase in cost of books and literature explosion. They also criticised that no follow up had been done, and that the State Governments did not comply with these recommendations of the Commissions and therefore, did not provide adequate grant for the library development.

2.5.4. Ranganathan Committee on Library Science in Indian Universities (1965)

The existing curriculum of most universities isbased on the recommendation of the Ranganathan Committee and the committee set up by the UGC in 1978. The recommendations made by these committees where mainly for bachelors level courses, which are outdated and irrelevant in the present day. In the 1980s, a marked change in LIS education programmes was required due to the introduction of information technology into the field. As a result, the next revision was initiated by the UGC in the early 1990s (Ranganathan 1965, Mahapatra 2006).

2.5.5. Mehrotra Committee (1983)

The UGC appointed a Committee on December 24, 1983 under the Chairmanship of Professor R.C.Mehrotra, Emeritus Professor, Rajasthan University, Jaipur to consider the revision of pay scales, career/professional development and service conditions of teachers in the universities and colleges. In October 1985, the UGC in consultation with the Government of India, requested the Mehrotra Committee to consider the revision of pay scales of Librarians and Directors of Physical Education too. The Committee submitted the report on revision of pay scales of Librarians to the UGC on September 3, 1986.

Recognising the importance of libraries in imparting and disseminating knowledge, the Mehrotra Committee discussed the functions of librarians in ever changing scenario in the field of library and information science and use of modern innovative information and communication technologies. The Committee's recommendations to revise pay scales of the librarians at various levels considering duties assigned to them are commensurate with the qualifications and improvement in quality of library services. The librarians should have promotional opportunities, adequate facilities to improve their qualifications or attend refresher courses to update their knowledge and new courses to impart instruction on modern technological developments.

The Committee discussed at length the qualifications for the recruitment of librarians. In order to have wider choice, M.Phil and Ph.D. were not made as an essential qualification for recruitment, but qualifying National Eligibility Test in Library and Information Science for the lecturers, assistant librarians, documentation officers and college librarians was made essential for improving the quality of new entrants. Librarians also needed to prepare self-assessment report at the end of each financial year. Assessment by users of the library should be considered important while assessing librarian's performance. The promotion of librarians should be linked with the acquisition of additional qualifications. The Committee suggested that librarians should be given duty leave to avail opportunities to attend summer schools, workshops, seminars, etc., to keep them abreast with the modern developments. The Government of India accepted the recommendations of the Mehrotra Committee and issued orders for the implementation of revised pay scales and qualifications for teachers in universities and colleges vide document No. F.1-21/

87-U.I dated 22nd July 1988. The recommendations regarding scales of pay, career advancement, promotion, terms and conditions of revised scales, recruitment and qualification requirements, continuing education and appraisal of performance, service conditions including period of probation, non-vacation, age of superannuation, code of professional ethics, grievances redressal mechanism and pay fixation formula were to be modified suitably for the librarians at different levels considering duties assigned to them. On 20th February 1990, document No.F.1-9/89 (CPP-I) regarding "Qualifications and Grades of Librarians" was issued in suppression of the previous Office Circular No. F.1-96/81 (CP/MP) dated 31st August 1984. The minimum qualifications for recruitment of various posts of librarians were revised consequent upon the revision of pay scales with effect from 1st January 1986. Since then, universities and colleges are advertising the posts with revised pay scales and revised qualifications for the recruitment of Librarian, Deputy Librarian, Assistant Librarian, Documentation Officer and College Librarian.

2.5.6. Committee on National Network System for Universities / Libraries (1988)

The Planning Commission had set up a Working Group on Modernisation of Library Services and Informatics for the Seventh Five Year Plan (1985-90) under the Chairmanship of Dr.N.Seshagiri, Additional Secretary, and Department of Electronics. The Working Group suggested developing a computer network interlinking all special libraries in India by 2000 A.D. In 1988, the UGC constituted a Committee on National Network System under the Chairmanship of Prof. Yash Pal, the then UGC Chairman to suggest measures for networking of libraries and information centres in universities, deemed universities, institutions of national importance, UGC Information Centres, R&D institutions and colleges. The main objective of the Committee was to share the existing resources to optimise utilisation and avoid duplications of holdings so as to have an access to wide range of literature.

In the first meeting on April 24, 1988, the Committee decided to constitute a Working Group to prepare a project report on 'Information and Library Network' (INFLIBNET) within three months. The members of the Working Group were experts and officials of some representative organisations, libraries, information centres, computer and communication fields, etc. They commenced their work on June 2, 1988 and completed the assignment on August 31, 1988; the role of UGC and other bodies in promoting libraries in universities, colleges and other institutions of higher learning.

The Working Group referred to the views of the policy documents such as:

- Scientific Policy Resolution and Technology Policy Statement;
- National Policy on Education; and
- Proposed National Policy on Library and Information System.

It also recognised various efforts already made and being planned in the country for modernising of libraries and information centres and the developmental programmes of NISSAT, NIC, DESINET, ERNET, CALIBNET, DELNET and the CSIRNET. The Working Group covered in detail various aspects such as output and services, INFLIBNET organisation, standardisation for information handling, application software requirements, computer hardware, technical specialisations, network manpower and training need, management mechanism, implementation mechanism and cost implications.

2.5.7. Curriculum Development Committee on Library and Information Science (1990-93)

The UGC initiated the scheme of restructuring of courses during Seventh Plan period to make education relevant to the needs of the community. A number of Curriculum Development Centres were set up in 1986 to review the existing syllabi and to suggest measures for modernising unit model courses. On March 27, 1989 Curriculum Development Centres were in operation and model curriculum of 20 disciplines was developed. The efforts were made to make education socially relevant and meaningful considering modern trends in development of each discipline. Many universities and colleges have adopted newly structured courses. To bring a uniform national pattern to LIS education in India, the UGC appointed the Curriculum Development Committee (CDC) in 1990 to restructure the curriculum under the chairmanship of Prof. P.N. Kaula. The report of this committee was published in 1993 under the title "Report of the curriculum development committee on library & information science" (Kaula, 1993). The publication of this curriculum helped university departments update their syllabi; however, the report was found unsatisfactory and was not adopted by most universities (Mahapatra 2006).

The CDC sent questionnaires to 69 departments of Library and Information Science for collecting information about the curricula followed for imparting instruction in LIS courses and other related aspects. The responses to the questionnaires were received from 24 universities. The CDC conducted five meetings between December 1990 and January 1992 and two workshops on February 12,1991 and March 19,1993. The participants of the workshops were either practicing librarians of various institutions or teachers from the departments of LIS of several universities.

The Committee gave a historical overview of the development of LIS education in independent India and the present status of LIS education. The CDC suggested some guidelines to LIS schools, regarding admission policy, criteria for admission test, student strength, work experience, medium and methods of instruction, use of teaching aids and so on. The committee further emphasised provision of minimum accommodation for the department of LIS, setting up of the library and workshop- cum-information processing laboratory, strength of teaching and non-teaching staff and recruitment of teachers following prescribed qualifications by UGC. The most important contribution of the committee was the formulation of new curricula with core courses and optional courses. Referring to the recommendations of the UGC Review Committee (1965) and the UGC Panel of LIS (1982), CDC reiterated the establishment of separate Library and Department of LIS at every university. The CDC also emphasised the need for creation of more posts of professors in LIS—at least one post of Professor for each University offering MLIS course. The CDC further recommended a minimum full-time teaching faculty and at least a Reader to head the Department of Library and Information Science. The scenario of the Library and Information Science is changing rapidly in India. The UGC has launched INFLIBNET. Many academic and special libraries have started using various modern sophisticated information and communication technologies for computerisation of library operations and services, CD-ROM and other international databases, reprographic and micrographic equipment as well as local area and wide area networks. All these factors warrant revision of curriculum and adopting new educational teaching aids to make teaching more effective and produce sufficient library and information personnel well-versed in use of the equipment to provide effective services. The CDC therefore, has recommended strengthening LIS departments by providing:

- initial lump-sum grant of Rs. 25 lakhs for acquiring basic equipment;
- PC-AT or PC-XT and one lakh rupees for acquiring suitable software; and
- guidelines to universities to treat LIS departments along with other science departments for allocation of equipment grants.

2.5.8. Rastogi Committee (1997- 1998)

The UGC appointed a Committee in 1997 under the Chairmanship of Prof.R.P.Rastogi to consider the revision of pay scales and career advancement of the academic staff of the universities and colleges. On the recommendations of the Rastogi Committee, the Ministry of Human Resource Development announced the revised pay scales of the teachers, librarians and physical instructors vide its letter No. 1-22/97-U.1 dated July 27, 1998. The Ministry issued subsequent clarifications vide its notification No. 1-22/97-U.1 dated March 24, 1999 while retaining parity of pay scales of librarians with teachers, it withdrew the parity in terms of career advancement, re-employment or extension of service and fixation of pay scales, etc. These anomalies and discrepancies are mentioned below:

- **Parity :** The Deputy and Assistant Librarians are considered at par with the administrative staff namely Deputy and Assistant Registrar respectively.
- **Career Advancement Scheme :** According to Mehrotra Committee, the Assistant Librarian in the pay scale of Rs. 2200-4000 was eligible for the senior scale of Rs. 3000-5000 on completion of 8 years of service and was eligible for selection grade after 16 years of service as Assistant Librarian. In case of Ph.D. holders the time span was reduced to 6 years for senior scale and 13 years for selection grade as in the case of lecturers. There was also further additional increment for those who are holding M.Phil./Ph.D. degree. The scheme is still effective for teachers and is made more attractive but the Ministry of HRD vide its letter dated March 24, 1999 has scrapped the provision in case of librarians.
- **Age of Superannuation :** The age limit for the retirement of teachers and university librarians is extended to 62 years but the same has been denied to Deputy and Assistant Librarians.
- **Re-employment and Extension :** The scheme of re-employment and extension after retirement at the age of 62 years continues for Teachers but not for the Deputy and Assistant Librarians.
- **Pay Fixation for Deputy Librarians :** Deputy Librarians enjoy the parity of pay scales with Readers but have been denied the benefit of pay fixation at Rs. 14,940 after completion of five years of service.
- **Work Experience for Direct Recruitment :** There is disparity in regard to work experience for direct recruitment to the post of University Librarian. A Reader with work experience of 10 years is eligible for direct recruitment to the post of University Professor whereas in case of Deputy Librarian, it is raised to 13 years of work experience for direct recruitment to the position of University Librarian. Librarians have represented

their case and are pursuing with the Ministry as well as the UGC to restore the complete parity by removing these anomalies and treat them at par with the teachers for everything. But no decision has been taken yet. It is still under process and librarians are hopeful of getting the parity restored.

2.5.9. Karisiddappa Committee on Curriculum Development in Library and Information Science (2001)

The UGC constituted Subject Panels in different disciplines, including for Library and Information Science (LIS) courses vide its letter No. F.2-13/97 dated April 2, 1997 with Prof.C.R.Karisidappa as its convener to formulate model curriculum and prepare the status report with modifications of existing guidelines where necessary. The Panel of LIS had its first meeting in Karnataka University, Dharwad on March 10-11, 1998, after the meeting of conveners of all disciplines with Dr. Hari Gautam, Chairman, UGC on July 24, 1997. The plan for preparing the Status Report and Model Syllabus in LIS was discussed in a couple of meetings of the Panel. The Committee conducted a survey of LIS education in India to collect information regarding current syllabus and other details by circulating a questionnaire to all the Department of LIS. Four separate Zonal Meetings were held at Kurukshetra University (November 12-13, 1998), Utkal University (December 9-10, 1998), Osmania University (December 29-30, 1998) and North Eastern Hill University (April 13-14, 1999). Meanwhile, two letters from the Chairman, UGC (F.4-1/1997 of March 8, 2000 and August 31, 2000) advised to constitute three groups of eight members each for the preparation of CDC Report. These three groups met at the UGC office on October 23-25, 2000, December 4-6, 2000 and January 8-10, 2001 respectively and finalised courses, modules, model syllabus, marks pattern, teaching hours and credits for every course. The Subject Panel examined in detail certain sources in their endeavour to prepare the Report. They were:

- UGC Library Committee Report on University and College Libraries, 1957 (under Dr.S.R.Ranganathan);

- UGC Review Committee Report on Library Science in Indian Universities, 1965 (under Dr.S.R.Ranganathan);
- UGC Report of the Review Committee - 1981 (appointed in 1979);
- UGC Report of Curriculum Development Committee in LIS - 1992 (Committee appointed in 1990 under the Chairmanship of Prof.P.N.Kaula);
- UNESCO Curriculum for Information Society, 1998;
- Recommendations of the Seminar on Training of LIS professionals in Germany and India with special focus on Information Technology (December 11-13, 2000, New Delhi);
- Minutes of various meetings of the Subject Panel on LIS including those with Conveners of Board of Studies of different universities in India; and
- Status Report prepared by the Subject Panel on the basis of survey of Departments of LIS in India, 2000.

The Panel suggested integrated approach to LIS education with a two year Master's Degree curriculum giving freedom to individual university to opt for one year BLIS and one year MLIS model. The integrated model has been recommended to provide adequate time for automation and information technology components and their application in various operations of a library. The Panel has adopted Modular Approach in formation of the Model Syllabus. It has proposed seven modules. These modules are further categorised into papers to be taught in 2-year plan with clear indications of theory and practical components. The Report also specifies number of hours for teaching each paper, with break-up of hours used for teaching, practical, assignments and seminars. The Report has also considered LIS education through distance mode and has suggested modifications to existing norms and standards formulated by the Distance Education Council (DEC, IGNOU). This Report will certainly be very useful for Board of Studies of Departments of LIS in Indian universities in planning and revising their syllabus and teaching strategies.

Recommendations of Karisiddappa Committee 2001

Karisiddappa Committee has given some recommendations towards development of LIS education in India (UGC, India, 2001).

Summary of Recommendations

1. Course Pattern : Marked emphasis is required to be laid on two years integrated course, which, at one hand can ensure eliminating duplication of course content when is presently imbibed in truncated BLISc and MLISc programmes, and on the other hand it will provide necessary time for teaching of Automation and Information Technology component and their application to library work.

University Departments desirous of running the truncated BLISc and MLISc courses may continue to run the same for some time but should also try to shift to the Integrated MLISc course in the phased manner in a reasonable time. In addition to the integrated MLISc course, the Universities may also consider to start different levels of courses in Library and Information Science.

2. Curricular Structure : The committee after prolonged deliberations with the concerned and taking into consideration the international scenario has considered the Modular approach to curriculum as a flexible structure to be adopted by the departments with varying levels of infrastructure facilities. Hence it is recommended that the individual departments may draw the content of the syllabus based on the modules with a ratio of 80:20 i.e., 80% from the modules and 20% emphasizing the local needs.

The LIS being an interdisciplinary subject is finding applications in different subject fields like commerce, business, industries, health science and technology, social studies and so on. To meet the requirements of manpower in these fields relevant specializations in the form of electives be offered.

The committee considered seriously the courses in LIS be more practical oriented and also expected that the students would come out with substantial gain after completing the courses. It is therefore necessary that the suggested course pattern with regard to distribution of marks for theory and practical, teaching hours and the number of credits be adopted by the departments.

3. Infrastructure : The department of LIS should be equipped with adequate number of practical tools in the traditional subjects such as classification schedules, catalogue codes, list of Subject Headings and Thesauri in the ratio of 1:2 (*i.e* one set of tools for two students).

The library should also provide for a good collection of Reference Sources and tools (both in print and electronic media) of all varieties to acquaint the students with sufficient knowledge of their use.

The curriculum emphasizes intensive as well as extensive practical knowledge on the use of IT applied to Library and Information Science. The departments should be equipped adequately in order to enable the students to acquire the knowledge and skills in the use of IT tools and services. For this purpose an IT laboratory with network facilities be established in the department with user terminals at the ratio of 1:5 (i.e., one terminal for every five students), This should be supported with all the standard software packages including one or two library application software packages.

In the changing scenario the teaching staff requirements suggested by two earlier reports viz., Dr. Ranganathan Committee Report of 1965 and Prof. Kaula Committee CDC Report of 1992 be taken as the basis for further improvement. Considering the imperative need on practical component especially in the IT area of growing specialization, the staff strength may be increased proportionately.

The existing facility for training of teachers available through Academic Staff Colleges in the Universities be appropriately restructured in purpose and content It was felt appropriate to avail the existing facilities with a renewed approach to enable the teachers to acquire the required knowledge and skill in IT so as to impart effectively to the students.

It is also felt that similar training facilities available through the UGC established centers i.e. INFLIBNET, NCSI and some selective University departments be involved in training the LIS teachers. This will amount to the optimum utilization of the facilities in these centers.

4. Distance Education : The moduler approach may be adopted by the distance education programmes also in entirety and the syllabus either for the truncated programmes of one year each of BLISc. and MLISc or for two year integrated MLISc programme can also be drawn suitably. The committee reviewed the norms and standards proposed by the DEC and suggested number of modification to the said. These modified norms and standards be adopted by all the Universities offering Distance mode LIS education.

Model Syllabus of LIS (2 Years Integrated MLIS Course)

Karisiddappa Committee has recommended 2 years MLIS integrated course instead of 1 year BLIS and 1 year MLIS courses (UGC, India, 2001). The detail of the model syllabus recommended by Karisiddappa Committee is given below.

Paper-I: Foundations of Library and Information Science

Unit-1 : Library as a Social institution

- Social and historical foundations of Library
- Different types of Libraries -their distinguishing features and functions
- Role of Library in formal and informal education

Unit-2 : Normative Principles of Library and Information Science

- Five Laws of Library Science
- Implications of Five Laws in Library and Information Activities

Unit-3 : Library Development

- Development of Libraries with special reference to India
- Resource Sharing and Library Networking

Unit-4 : Laws relating to Libraries and Information

- Library legislation-need and essential features
- Library legislation in India
- Press and Registration Act and Delivery of Books (Public Libraries) Act
- Copyright Act

Unit-5 : Library and Information Profession

- Attribution of profession
- Librarianship as a Profession
- Professional ethics
- Professional associations and their role
- National and International Library Associations
- Professional Education and Research

Unit-6 : Promoters of Library and Information Services

- National level promoters - RRRLF
- International level promoters -UNESCO

Unit-7 : Public Relations and Extension Activities

- Definition
- Facets and Programs
- Publicity and Extension, Outreach Activities
- Library Path Finders (Guides)
- Consultancy including Promotional Web Tools.

Paper-II : Knowledge Organisation, Information Processing & Retrieval (THEORY)

Unit -1 : Universe of Knowledge

- Structure and attributes
- Models of formation of subjects

- Different types of subjects
- Universe of subjects as mapped in different schemes of classification

Unit-2 : Bibliographic Description

- Catalogue-purpose, structure and types, physical forms including OPAC, Filing Rules
- Normative Principles of Cataloguing
- Overview of principles and practice in document description
- Current trends in standardisation, description and exchange
- Standard codes of cataloguing

Unit-3 : Methods of Knowledge Organisation

- General theory of Library classification
- Normative principles of classification and their application
- Species of Library classification
- Standard schemes of classifications and their features; CC, DDC, UDC
- Design and Development of schemes of Library Classification
- Trends in Library classification

Unit-4 : Subject Cataloguing

- Principles of Subject cataloguing
- Subject heading lists and their features

Paper-III : Knowledge Organisation, information Processing & Retrieval (PRACTICE)

Unit-1 : Classification of Documents (using at least one standard scheme)

- Classification of documents representing simple subject
- Classification of documents having common isolates
- Classification of documents representing compound subject

- Classification of documents representing complex subject

Unit-2 : Assignment of Book Number

(Using at least one standard Book Numbering System)

Unit -3 : Cataloguing of Documents

(using at least one standard cataloguing code)

- Cataloguing of simple documents
- Cataloguing of complex documents

Unit-4 : Subject Cataloguing

- Assigning Subject Headings using at least one Standard Subject Headings

Paper IV : Information Technology: Basics

PART-I : (THEORY)

Unit-1 : Information Technology

- Definition, Need, Scope and Objectives

Unit-2 : Computer Basic (Hardware)

- Historical development of computers
- Generations of Computers, Classification of Computers

Unit-3 : Computer Architecture- Organisation Computer

- Input and Output Devices

Unit-4 : Software

- Operating Systems: Single & Multi-user, Systems Basic features of MS-DOS, MS Windows, Linux, UNIX, WINDOWS-NT etc.
- Programming Languages: Concepts and Tools
- Algorithm & Flowcharting

Unit-5 : Word Processors, Spread Sheets etc.

Unit-6 : DBMS Packages

- dBASE, FOXPro, CDS/ISIS, MS Access (Basic features)

PART-II: (PRACTICE)

Unit-1 Use of Operating Systems

Unit-2 Word Processor Spread Sheets

Unit-3 Database Creation using at least one DBMS Software

Unit-4 Database Search and Retrieval

Paper-V: Management of Library and Information Centres/ Institutions

Unit-1 : Management

- Concept; definition and scope
- Management styles and approaches
- Management schools of thought
- Functions and Principles of Scientific Management.

Unit-2 : Human Resource Management

- Organisational Structure
- Delegation, Communication and Participation
- Job Description and Analysis; Job evaluation
- Inter-personal Relations
- Recruitment Procedures
- Motivation; Group Dynamics
- Training and Development
- Disciplines and Grievances
- Performance Appraisal

Unit-3 : Financial Management

- Resource Mobilisation

- Budgeting Techniques and Methods-PPBS, Zero Based Budgeting etc.
- Budgetary Control
- Cost Effectiveness and Cost Benefit Analysis
- Outsourcing

Unit-4 : Reporting

- Types of Reports, Annual Report-Compilation, Contents and Style
- Library Statistics etc.

Unit-5 : System Analysis and Design

- Library as a System
- Project Management, PERT\CPM
- Decision Tables
- Performance Evaluation Standards, MIS
- Performance Measurement, Reengineering, Time and Motion Study
- SWOT (Strength, Weakness, Opportunities, Threat)
- DFD (Data Flow Diagram)

Unit-6 : Total Quality Management (TQM)

- Definition, Concept, Elements
- Quality Audit, LIS related standards
- Technology Management

Unit-7 : Library House Keeping Operations

- Different Sections of Library & Information Centre and their functions
- Collection Development and Management Policies, Procedures
- Book ordering(Acquisition)
- Technical Processing

- Serials Control, Circulation Control, Maintenance etc.
- Stock Verification-Policies and Procedures
- Evaluation and weeding
- Archiving-Conservation - Preservation
- Restoration including Print, Non-print and Electronic Materials

Unit-8 : Planning

- Concept, Definition, Need and Purpose; Types
- Policies and Procedures, MBO
- Building and Space Management in Libraries and Information Centres
- Risk Management, Contingency Management
- Planning of Related Infrastructure, Library Standards

Unit-9 : Management of Change

- Concept of Change
- Changes in procedures, Methods, Tools and Techniques
- Problems of Incorporating Change
- Techniques of Managing Change

Paper VI: Information Sources and Services (THEORY)

Unit-1 : Reference and Information Sources

- Documentary Sources of Information ;Print non print including Electronic
- Nature, characteristics, utility and evaluation of different types of Information Sources
- Non Documentary Information Sources
- Human and Institutional; Nature types, characteristics and utility

- Categories: Primary, Secondary and Tertiary information Sources
- Internet as a Source of Information

Unit-2 : Reference Service

- Concept, Definition and Trends
- Reference Interview and Search Techniques

Unit-3 : Information Users and their Information Needs

- Categories of Information Users
- Information Needs: Definition and Models
- Information Seeking Behaviour
- User Studies: Methods, Techniques and Evaluation

Unit-4 : Information Services and Products

- Information Services and Product
- Information Services: Concepts, Definition, Need and Trends
- Need, Techniques and Evaluation of Alerting Services (CAS & SDI)
- Bibliographic, Referral, Document Delivery and Translation Services

Unit-5 : Information Systems and their Services

- Study of National, International and Commercial Information Systems and Services
- Background, their Services and Products

Unit-6 : User Education

- Goals and objectives.
- Levels, Techniques and Methods, Evaluation of Users
- Educational Programmes,

Paper-VII : Information Sources and Services

(PRACTICE)

Unit-1 : Study and evaluation of Information Sources

Unlt-2 : Compilation of current awareness list / bibliography / contents list / Press Clippings

Paper VIII: Library and Users

PART-I: THEORY

Unit-1 : Techniques of Library and information Centres Survey

- Proforma method
- Interview Method
- Records analysts method

Unit-2 : Information Users and their Information Needs

- Categories of Information Users
- Information Needs-definition and models
- Information Seeking Behaviour

Unit-3 : User Studies

- Methods and techniques of User studies
- Evaluation of User Studies

PART-2: PRACTICE

Unit-1 : Survey of Libraries and Information Centres Unit-2 Survey of a group of Users

Paper IX: Information and Communication

Unit-1 : Information and Communication

- Information; Characteristics, Nature, Value and Use of Information

- Conceptual difference between Data, Information and Knowledge
- Communication of Information: Information generation
- Communication channels, models and barriers
- Trends in Scientific Communication

Unit-2 : Information Science

- Definition, Scope and Objectives
- Information Science as a discipline and its relationship with other subjects

Unit-3 : Library, information and Society

- Genesis and characteristics and implications of Information Society
- Changing role of Library and Information Centres in Society
- Information Industry-Generators, Providers and Intermediaries
- Intellectual Property Act, Right to Information Acts
- Concept of freedom, censorship, data security and fair use
- Policies relating to information, Right to Information including science and technology, education
- International and National Programmes and Policies (NAPLIS) IT and Library UAP, UBC

Unit-4 : Economics of Information

Unit-5 : Information Management

Unit-6 : Knowledge Management

Paper X: Information Analysis, Repackaging and Consolidation

Unit-1 Abstracting

- **Abstracting :** Types and guidelines in preparing Abstract

Unit-2 : Repackaging and Consolidation

- Content Analysis
- Repackaging, formatting, consolidation

Unit-3 : Information Products

- Information Products: Nature, Concept, Types, Design; and Development and Marketing.

Unit-4 : Trends in Information Analysis, Repackaging and Consolidation, including Electronic Content Creation

Paper XI: Information Retrieval

PART-1: THEORY

Unit-1 : Cataloguing & Subject Indexing: Principles and Practices

- Principles of Subject Cataloguing: Assigning Subject headings Using Library of Congress Subject Headings and Sear's List of Subject Headings etc.
- Models-Assigned and Derived
- Pre & Post Coordinate Indexing Systems and Citation indexing

Unit-2 : Indexing Languages and Vocabulary Control

- Indexing Languages: Types and Characteristics
- Vocabulary Control
- Tools of Vocabulary Control
- Structure and construction of an IR Thesaurus
- Trends in Automatic Indexing

Unit-3 : Information Retrieval

- IR Models, Search Strategies; Manual /Machine, Feedback and Refining
- Evaluation of Information Retrieval Systems; Projects and Parameters

- Trends in IR Models

PART 2 : PRACTICE

Unit-1 Assigned Indexing Practice

Unit-2 Derived Indexing Practice

Unit-3 Design and development of IR Thesaurus

Unit-4 Search Methods and Formulation of Search Strategy

Paper XII: Research Methods and Statistical Techniques

Unit-1 : Research

- Concept, Meaning, Need and process of Research
- Types of Research -Fundamental and Applied including inter disciplinary and multidisciplinary approach
- Research and Development of Scholarship

Unit-2 : Research Design

- Conceptualisation and operationalisation
- Types of Research Design
- Identification and formulation of problem
- Hypothesis; Nominal and Operational definition
- Designing Research Proposal
- Ethical aspects of Research
- Literature search -Print, Non-print and Electronic sources

Unit-3 : Research Methods

- Scientific Method
- Historical Method
- Descriptive Method
- Survey Method and Case Study Method
- Experimental Method and Delphi Method

Unit-4 : Research Techniques and Tools

- Questionnaire
- Schedule
- Interview
- Observation
- Scales and check lists
- Library Records and Reports
- Sampling Techniques

Unit-5 : Data Analysis and interpretation

- Descriptive Statistics-Measures of Centra! Tendency; Mean, Mode, Median
- Tabulation and Generalisation
- Measures of dispersion, variance and covariance
- Standard Deviation
- Graphical presentation of data-bar, pie-line graphs, histograms etc.
- Inferential Statistics
- Z-T test-Correlation
- Regression-linear and non-linear
- Chi Square Test
- Sociometry
- Statistics Packages-SPSS
- Statistical Graphics etc.

Unit-6 : Bibliometrics, Scientometrics, and tnformetrics

- Concept and Definition
- Bibliometric Laws; Bradford; Zipf, Lotka
- Bibliographic Coupling
- Obsolescence
- Citation Analysis

- Webometrics
- Citation Studies
- Infometrics
- Scientomatrics

Unit-7 : Research Reporting

- Structure, Style, Contents
- Guidelines for Research Reporting
- Style Manuals-Chicago -MLA -APA etc.
- e-Citation and Methods of Research Evaluation

Unit-8 : Current Trends in Library and information Science Research

Paper XIII: Information Technology: Applications

Unit-1 : Library Automation

- Planning and Implementation and Library Automation
- Automation, In-house operations-Acquisition, Cataloguing, Circulation, Serials Control, OPAC, Library Management

Unit-2 : Mufti Lingual Bibliographic Databases

- Library Automation Software Packages; their study and composition

Unit-3 : Communication Technology

- Fundamentals of Telecommunication Technology; Media, Mode and Components
- Network Media, UTP, Optical Fibre, Ethernet, Network interface card, Hubs, Routers, Modern
- Network Types and Topologies, LAN, WAN, MAN
- Bus, Star, Ring, Token Ring, etc.
- Local Area Network- Types and Topologies

Unit-4 : INTERNET Basic features and Tools

- Network Based Information Services
- Connectivity: Dial-up, Leased lines, ISDN, Digital subscriber lines
- E-Mail, SMTP, Wireless, Send mail, POP3 CK
- Protocols- FTP, HTTP
- Web browser; Netscape Navigator, Internet Explorer
- Web Servers, Web tools, Search Engines
- Internet Security
- Teleconferencing, Tele-facsimile, Teletex, Videotext

Unit-5 : Digital Libraries

- Genesis, Definition, Objectives, Scope of Digital Libraries
- Image formats, Audio formation
- Storage media Formats-18 0-9660 DVD
- Software and Hardware for digital libraries, OCR, Image Editing software
- Input capture devices, scanners, digital, movie cameras
- Data Warehousing, Data Mining and Meta Data

Unit-6 Artificial Intelligence & Expert Systems

(with reference to Library & Information Science)

Paper XIV : Information Technology: Applications (PRACTICE)

Unit-1 : Creation and Maintenance of Databases by CDS/ ISIS and others

Unit-2 : Using of Library Software Packages

Unit-3 : CD-ROM, Online searching

Unit-4 : Internet Searching

Unit-5 : Library and Information Centre Web page design and creation

Paper XV: Electives : Information Systems

An illustrative list of Electives option is as under. It is not suggestive but illustrative

1. Business Information System
2. Environmental Information System
3. Biotechnology Information Systems
4. Health Science Information Systems
5. Archival, Museum and Archaeological Information Systems
6. Legal Information Systems
7. Agricultural Information Systems
8. Social Sciences Information Systems
9. Industrial Information Systems
10. Rural and Community Information Systems

Note: The Electives are offered in Semester IV, MLISc-II or MLISC; as Paper 15 with the following broad structure of contents:-

1. Study of the specialised subject/discipline- its structure and development
2. Definition, Terminology, Branches and Landmarks in the subject/disciplines
3. Planning, Design and Evaluation of Information Systems
4. Database design, creation and development in the area- pertaining to information components of the subject, study of Data Structure, selection of DBMS and Retrieval aspects, Content Creation and Development
5. Information Systems and Networks in the subject/discipline, Study of Information Sources Services, Internet-based Sources & Services,

2.6. ONLINE AND VIRTUAL LEARNING IN LIS EDUCATION

The introduction of ICT has drastically changed the LIS teaching paradigm. In the age of Internet and web 2.0, the LIS education is becoming more user friendly and interactive. Various efforts towards implementing online and virtual learning in LIS are briefly described (Ramesha and Asundi, 2011):

(a) **Early Efforts**

The role of computers in education was clearly identified in the mid-1980s as a tool for extended teaching and learning facilitator. The early efforts were mostly confined to standalone environment in the form of packages developed using programming languages like BASIC. The "Authoring Languages" created a new view on computerized teaching methods. One expert has experimented the use of BASIC Programming Language to create a learning package for the teaching of Library Classification and the presented it as LEARDDC in the Seminar organized by the Indian Statistical Institute, (DRTC). Bangalore in the year 1989. However the use of Authoring Languages served as mode of question-answer presentations and learning was simple and effective.

The authoring languages PILOT and TUTOR popular in 1980s are responsible for the design of varieties of learning modules termed as;

(i) Computer Aided Learning (CAL)

(ii) Computer Based Learning (CCL)

(iii) Computer Managed Instruction (CMI)

(iv) Computer Aided Instruction (CAI)

(v) Computer Assisted Learning (CAL)

(vi) Computer-Based Learning (CBI)

(vii) Intelligent Tutoring System (ITS)

The authoring languages in a conversational or dialogue style showes how learning is programmed with their use. The CAI packages were also developed with BASIC programming language, which has the interactive character, but it was found easier to use PILOT than BASIC.

The optical storage devices augmented multimedia products

which are popular even today in teaching and in self-instructional systems. They found good applications in industry (for product catalogues, databases, directories) and in libraries They were incidentally first to hiring a change in teaching and learning as they focused on enhancement of learning because of the convergence of several media and with simultaneous and concurrent presentations.

(b) Online Tutorials

The late 1960s and early 1970s, saw the advent of a new information scenario-the Online Information Services. The pioneers are Bibliographic Retrieval Services (BRS), Online Retrieval of Bibliographic Information Timeshared (ORBIT) and the DIALOG The DIALOG introduced "Online Training and Practice Modules" (ONTAP) for the information services offered by them and used in training the users and the information facilitators. The packages formed integral part of every IRS.

(c) Content Management Systems (CMS)

The digital environment set in a new wave in education, teaching and research. This was coupled with processing speed, mass storage devices and real-time retrieval The Internet and WWW were instrumental in innovative technologies furthered by Free Open Source Software (FOSS). This trend made a beginning for the Content Management Systems (CMS) which performed multifarious tasks, like administration, access, search, updating, assessment and evaluation. The Drupal one of the CMS also fostered collaboration in enterprise content management and sharing of resources.

(d) E-Learning Packages and OCW

The E-learning open source software like Moodle, Manhattan and Brihaspati on the broad perception of content access and delivery in a web-based learning system have adapted many features of a virtual class room and consisted of common modules ;

(i) Administrator's Interface

(ii) Instructor Interface

(iii) Student interface

The Learning Management Systems and the Learning Objects were also part of these packages. The e-learning descended a new era with built in teaching, learning, assessment and evaluation concepts. The perceptions of teaching largely changed with these developments, where the shift was from teacher centered to machine interface centered pedagogy. This eventually offered varieties of learning modes like; online, e-correspondence, access to virtual class room, interactive multimedia and so on. The success of these developments is supported by the Open Course Ware (OCW).

(e) Virtual Learning

The implementation of e-learning is possible in two ways -on stand alone platform and web-based. In contrast virtual learning is different as it provides for real-time, live and individualistic learning. It combines virtual class room with facilities for video conferencing using high-end communication networks, both wired and wireless, The Hughes Net and EDUSAT are employed in virtual learning via VSAT connectivity. The Ministry of Information Technology, Government of India has Launched many projects for the human resource development in order to promote IT in education. This has been explicitly given in the Annual Reports of the Ministry (http://mit.gov.in). The EDUSAT has now extended its teaching learning facilities to the Primary and Secondary Education levels as well as at the professional courses of a university as presented by the Visveswaraya Technological University, Belgaum.

The applications of ICT in education, teaching and delivery of content have been achieved in a very logical and progressive manner. The perception of the users seems to be positive and encouraging in all these instances which have endeavored to employ learners perceptions to assimilate the content delivered to them, either through the words of mouth or through machine interface, static, dynamic and/or live.

2.7. PROBLEMS IN LIS EDUCATION IN INDIA

Library Science programmes at the university level have existed for more than six decades and have strong roots, but the profession still suffers from many problems, which are affecting the status of LIS profession. The most important is an urgent need for a national level accreditation body. Not much has been done, even with the establishment of the National Assessment and Accreditation Council (NAAC). There is a need that all the organizations running LIS courses without adequate facilities be abandoned. Other problems requiring discussion by the UGC and other national level professional bodies are discussed below:

(a) Accreditation

To achieve academic excellence, it is of utmost importance that standards and norms of education be prescribed and adherence to them be made mandatory. Unfortunately, there is no national accreditation body for LIS education in India. As a result, new LIS schools are opening at a fast pace following different patterns of education and without the basic minimum facilities, resulting in mass production of professionals with sub-standard education and having least or no exposure to practical librarianship. In principle, no new LIS school should be established without the approval of such an accreditation agency. This agency should be responsible for recommending minimum standards in terms of faculty strength, intake criteria, teacher-student ratio, evaluation methods, library and laboratory facilities, availability of teaching materials, finance and physical facilities, etc. It should also take care of regular revision of LIS syllabi for uniformity and standardization in the overall LIS education system which is presently missing. Although the UGC, through its LIS Committee has revised and recommended the syllabi for BLIS and MLIS courses, these are not followed by most of the universities as the role of the UGC is more recommending in nature rather than accrediting. As a result, each university is designing its own curriculum, follows its own practices, and resulting in wide disparities among programmes. National associations have also made sincere efforts by holding conferences and seminars and discussing vital issue of accreditation. Unfortunately, nothing concrete have been done so far. In 1976, IFLA in its annual conference passed a resolution that "to maintain uniformity in the standards in the LIS Education programmes in the country, the Government of India be requested to create a Library Science Council on the pattern of Indian Medical Council" (Baba, 1999, p.570). In 1994, the Nagpur University organized a UGC sponsored national seminar on Accreditation of Library and Information Science Schools in India. This seminar also emphasized the need for establishing an independent National Council to be named as the Indian Council for Accreditation of Library and Information Science Education (ICALISE) similar to the American Library Association in USA and the Library Association in UK, as well as the Indian Medical Council Act, Bar Council of India Act and All India Council for Technical Education Act.

(b) Mushrooming of Library Schools

There is no check and balance on the emergence of new LIS schools; and this result in a large number of institutions emerging without offering the basic facilities. Emergence of such institutions has resulted in mass production of substandard library professionals and thus, creating an increasing problem of unemployment in the job market. In some universities, the trend of paid seats has started. The scenario in many universities that conduct distance education is not very promising as they do not have adequate number of teaching centres and computer laboratory, as well as feedback from students. This has resulted in a passive teaching-learning process. Competition in the job market is increasing day by day as production is much more than the demand.

(c) Inadequate Faculty Strength

Reputation of any course depends on the teaching standard which presupposes the adequate faculty strength with good academic record, up-to-date knowledge of the subject and adequate teaching experience. In earlier years, the UGC Review Committee (1965) rejected the practice of employing the university library staff as part-time teachers and recommended one reader and two lecturers for a department conducting BLIS programme, and one professor, two readers and four lecturers for a department conducting the MLIS. The Curriculum Development Committee (CDC) in 1992 recommended for a department running BLIS (having not more than 40 students) and MLIS (having not more than 15 students), one professor, one reader and three lecturers (1:1:3) and a provision should be made for one additional teacher for every 10 students after 40 for BLIS and 15 for MLIS.

(d) Lack of Library Facilities

Many LIS schools have either no library at all, or a library with inadequate collection of text-books, reference books and practical tools (classification schemes, cataloguing codes and list of subject headings). Availability of the latest editions of textboks and reference sources are altogether out of question. The library, for library science students is like a workshop or a laboratory to do practical assigments, learn and create new things. No library science school should be established without having an adequately equipped library, required for day to day practical classes.

(e) Information Technology Laboratory

The majority of the LIS schools, particularly after the submission of the CDC report in 1992, are offering courses on computer applications to prepare students for the electronic information environment; unfortunately most of the schools do not have well-equipped computer laboratory. Competent professionals cannot be produced with merely theoretical exposition; they require adequate practical exposure by working in a well-developed computer laboratory. Practical training for computerized routines such as house-keeping jobs, provision of information services, Internet access, Online and CD-ROM searching, etc, is required. UGC Model Curriculum Committee (2001) has strongly recommended that apart from enriching the contents, it is necessary that LIS departments have an

IT laboratory with network facilities. Terminal facility should be available in the ratio of 1:5 that is one computer terminal for every five students. The laboratory should be further supported with standard software packages including one or two library application software packages.

(f) Curriculum Revision

In many universities the LIS syllabi are quite old and they need to be restructured with redefined objectives to accommodate emerging changes in the libraries and expectations of users. Adoption of well-designed curricula will ensure quality education, resulting in quality products, suitable both for the practising librarianship as well as teaching staff. Presently there is a wide disparity in the courses, their duration, number and name of papers, contents, number of lectures and practical periods, methods of teaching and evaluation, and grading system. The period after 1980s has witnessed a great transition due to the impact of computer and communication technology which is responsible for the emergence of an 'Information Society' and 'Global Village'. Therefore, it has become essential that curricula be revised by reducing emphasis on teaching of traditional techniques and philosophical aspects to incorporate emerging areas such as computer and communication technology, knowledge management, information systems, information processing and retrieval systems, online information sources, and marketing of products and services. Revised curriculum should be capable of preparing the future professionals in order to meet the challenges enforced upon them from time to time.

(g) Admission Procedures and Intake

Admission criteria for any course should be based on sound principles relating to manpower requirements but this is not so in Indian LIS educational setting. UGC review committee report (1965, p.39) recommended the ratio between teacher and students at BLIS and MLIS to be 1:10 and 1: 15 respectively, which can ideally help to develop competent information professionals. But the ground reality is that in many schools, there is only one full-time teacher assisted by a few part-time teachers, teaching many courses up to Ph.D level. The teacherstudent ratio is high and this has resulted in large number of students graduating without adequate exposure to theory and practice, therefore producing graduates with sub-standard training as well as creating the problem of unemployment. A good profession is one which is capable of obtaining jobs before the announcement of examination results or immediately after the completion of the programme. This is possible today, if accreditation of LIS schools becomes essential, the number of schools and seats are kept limited, and the quality of education is maintained. Such situation would not only help raise the status of the profession but also provide a wider recognition and acceptance in the society. Therefore, for the qualitative manpower development, students intake should be given due importance keeping in view the needs of the job market.

(h) Students' Selection Criteria

Library and information science is slowly becoming popular, students with better qualifications are joining the course but they are not enthusiastic in opting for library science as their first choice. Therefore, more attention towards selection criteria is needed to attract the best brains. Even to attract middle level talent, incentives like scholarships and fellowships are needed. Merit (as in many universities) should not be the only criteria for admitting the students. Admission test and interview should be adopted to select appropriate students, with pleasant personality, good general knowledge, communication skill, inborn love for books, aptitude towards librarianship and desire to serve others.

(i) Apprenticeship Programme

All professional courses need adequate practical training as merely theoretical exposition in the classrooms do not make the students proficient to handle the live situations of practical librarianship. System of apprenticeship or practical training must become an essential component of the programme. Although some schools are adopting this practice, others should also take initiative to develop mutual understanding with the selected libraries for this purpose. A Memorandum of Understanding (MOU), with the libraries willing to accept the students for practical training, may be signed. Such training increase the competency building of the students and give them an opportunity to learn while they work. This would make them more confident and competent to face the challenges of librarianship when they enter the profession later.

(j) Dual Responsibility

In 1979, the UGC Panel on Library and Information Science recommended for the independent status to the LIS departments but in some states such as Maharashtra and Karnataka, professor of LIS is also in charge of the university library, thus, holding dual responsibility. This is not a healthy practice and is against the recommendation made by the panel.

2.8. TREND OF LIS EDUCATION IN ABROAD

In the changing context of electronic information environment, the library users especially the students are more accustomed with handling the digital information rather than the printed one. They feel more comfortable to search Yahoo, Google, OPAC, Portal, Subject Gateway etc through the ICT. Therefore library professional needs to be equipped with the current digital library technology to serve these types of users. Again keeping conformable relation to the users' needs and demands the curriculum in LIS School also have to be restructured. Like India, other parts of the world have also seriously discussed the matter to revise the LIS curriculum. In July 2000 a report from the W. K. Kellogg foundation was published examining the library and information science (LIS) curriculum. It was the most extensive examination since the 1923 Williamson Report. Called the KALIPER project – (the Kellogg-ALISE Information Professions and Education Renewal project –it was conducted between 1998 and 2000 by a team of twenty scholars from thirteen programs in the U.S., Canada and England.

The group analyzed the nature and extent of major curricular change in LIS education. Multiple methods were used to collect data, including surveys, case studies, content analysis and interviews. They concluded that there were six trends shaping curriculam change in LIS programs (Roegge, 2009).

Trend 1: In addition to libraries as institutions and library-specific operations LIS curricula are addressing broad-based information environments and information problems. Library schools, while still training students for more traditional library roles, are focusing on more digital information issues. Classes are offered that examine information products, licensing and copyright issues in a virtual environment and managing digital information. Cataloging courses are incorporating concepts such as metadata as well as more traditional classification schemes.

Trend 2: While LIS curricula continue to incorporate perspectives from other disciplines, a distinct core has taken shape that is predominantly user-centered. Courses in LIS programmes have traditionally been user-focused but the trend is for that aspect to be even more emphasized. "The emphasis on users is included in school mission and vision statements. Even system centered courses such as cataloging and data management, increasing incorporate the user paradigm". Because of this the faculty in many programs is becoming increasingly multidisciplinary.

Trend 3: LIS schools and programmes are increasing the investment and infusion of information technology into their curricula. Because today's libraries need to be on the cutting edge of technology LIS programmes are having to invest into the most up-to-date equipment and reconfigure space for computer labs. In these labs students learn about software applications, online searching, web design and other tasks related to an online environment. These labs also require trained staff to help maintain the equipment and assist in teaching.

Trend 4: LIS schools and programmes are experimenting with the structure of specialization within the curriculum. There has always been a discussion about specialization in library education. Programmes offer an option to focus on school media, medical, law, or archives. There seems to be a trend to provide fewer specializations and streamline the curriculum. Programmes are offering students options to customize their classes to their interests. They are looking at options such as dual-degrees with other schools on their campus, independent studies, internships and co-op programmes.

Trend 5: LIS schools and programs are offering instruction in different formats to provide students with more flexibility. More LIS programmes are offering courses online and through distance learning programmes. They are exploring other forms of instruction including inter-university partnerships, and collaboration with universities in other countries.

Trend 6: LIS Schools and programmes are expanding their curricula by offering related degrees at the undergraduate, master's and doctoral levels. Courses on information systems, management and studies are being offered at the undergraduate level. Master's programs are offering multiple degrees and new degrees are in the planning stage. The number of cross-listed courses are increasing.

A group of seven deans of LIS School gathered at the Institute of Museum and Library Services (IMLS) in Washington, DC, in August 2007 to discuss present and future demand for library and information science (LIS) professionals. They discussed topics include current research on the profession, trends in enrollment and placement, challenges and potential opportunities in LIS education, and strategies for capitalizing on the opportunities. Two background reports were provided as preparatory reading:

1. A 2006 research study by Jeffrey Pomerantz on Digital Library Education in Library and Information Science Programmes and
2. The report of a workshop convened in 2006 by IMLS and the Department of Canadian Heritage, "Canada-US Dialogue on Digital Cultural Heritage: Digital Readiness and Cultural Heritage Institutions." The reports together show increased

offerings on digital library topics within LIS programmes and increasing need for digital competencies and other professional skills among all types of cultural heritage institutions.

The summary of the meeting are categorized and given below (Institute of Museum and Library Services, Washington, DC, 2007):

Current Research

According to the research conducted by Jose-Marie Griffiths in 2004 :

- The demand for librarians continue to increase over the next decade as the current (aging) professional workforce retires.
- The employers are not eliminating positions when vacancies occur, and that new opportunities are arising both within and outside libraries for graduates with the skills that LIS programs provide.
- The study will provide an analysis of the current and projected U.S. library workforce by state and region, types of employers, and functional specializations, with data collection to be completed in fall 2007.
- Further, the study will assess the likely demand and opportunities for librarians over the next two decades, the skills they will need, the capacity of graduate LIS schools to meet projected needs, and incentives for attracting highly qualified individuals to the field.
- The report will recommend strategies for the recruitment, education, and retention of future librarians. Griffiths also described another IMLS-funded study underway at UNC Chapel Hill, directed by Joanne Marshall, which complements her own project.
- The Marshall study is tracing the career patterns of graduates from five LIS programmes in North Carolina over the past 30 years to better understand the educational, workplace, career and retention issues faced by LIS graduates.

Trends

As the discussion shifted towards the current environment and trends in LIS education, it is concluded that:

- The number of students enrolling in graduate LIS programmes is increasing and the average age of students is decreasing.
- More students are now coming directly into LIS programmes after receiving bachelor's degrees.
- Younger students are typically attracted to technology and to the "new library." Graduate students in LIS programmes, in addition to those in graduate museum studies and archival programs, want exposure to multiple digital and technology-related courses.
- Students generally do not want rigid limitations when choosing courses to meet curriculum requirements; they want a variety of choices and interdisciplinary options. The one exception seems to be in youth service areas such as school library media, where students tend to remain in that field without straying into other programmes.
- It is noted the particular interests of employers for graduates with strengths in taxonomy, policy, metadata management, financial information and information security. The museum studies students want access to technology courses offered in LIS programs and vice versa.
- Students are interested in both "the artifact" and in "digitizing the artifact," which conceptually links the concerns of museums and libraries through attention to archival principles.
- The similarities in professional skill sets needed to work in libraries, museums and archives as well the ways in which these institutions each function to preserve collections (including digital collections) and make them publicly accessible outweigh the differences.

Challenges

While participants agreed that the current trends, such as the broadening of students' interests, are positive, they noted that they also present problems. LIS graduates may have a solid grasp of technical skills upon entering the workforce but feel they are weak in business skills, "as if they want an MBA incorporated with their LIS." Although participants recognized good opportunities for collaboration with computer science departments, for example, they agreed that LIS programs cannot provide "informatics for everything." A common concern was that LIS programmes risk diluting their overall effectiveness and making little or no meaningful impact on the special interest topics. In addition, most institutions do not possess enough LIS faculty to extensively diversify their programs. Curricula by sharing courses and faculty among schools attracted a great deal of interest. Schools could build on the WISE (Web-based Information Science Education) distance education model, which IMLS has supported to provide sharing of LIS distance education courses among WISE consortium members; the NEH summer institute model; or the rare book school approaches at the University of Virginia and UCLA to provide faculty the opportunity to teach a specialized topic in more detail than is possible in regular LIS curricula. Students could come from other LIS schools to one summer institute location to learn about a specialized topic—cataloging, for example—taught by leaders in the field. This arrangement could also provide faculty members opportunities for visiting summer appointments, thus broadening their own experiences. Other related opportunities include Certificates of Advanced Study, either for continuing education programs for MLS graduates or for advanced LIS education for professionals coming into the field with other advanced degrees, and the establishment of post-doctoral programmes, in which students could gain teaching experience and which would provide incentives to enable more aggressive recruitment of faculty from LIS doctoral programmes and related fields.

Elizabeth Liddy, Syracuse University, noted that Professors of Practice, who typically are experienced library practitioners and are not tenure-track, can provide a good means of addressing students' needs for practical information. Their presence can also help schools satisfy accreditation requirements, and "students want what they bring."

All participants identified increasing the diversity of students and faculty as a goal. Jana Bradley, University of Arizona, noted the success of the Knowledge River programmes at her school, which is aimed at recruiting LIS students from Latino and American Indian communities. She identified an additional need for doctoral programmes to educate future faculty members from diverse backgrounds. As the demand for LIS education increases, along with the diversification of LIS programmes, the demand for additional, qualified LIS faculty grows. But as large schools diversify, the pool of faculty qualified to teach in certain LIS areas decreases. Likewise, schools that do not have doctoral LIS programmes have to rely for faculty on the schools that do have doctoral programmes. Other issues also contribute to the need for and availability of LIS educators, such as institutional barriers to hiring or the increasing number of job opportunities available to LIS graduates outside academia, either in libraries or in the private sector (in positions with information providers such as Google, Microsoft or Yahoo, for example).

Participants also discussed the development of information science as a distinct field within library education programmes and its effect on the educational community. Several mentioned that while membership in the I-School Caucus is restricted, the emphasis on information science is the direction in which virtually all LIS education is moving. The challenge will be for ALISE (Association of Library and Information Science Educators) and the I-Schools to keep the whole field involved in discussions about curriculum and other important issues, and to work together to maximize the sharing of resources and information. In that regard, the next two years of ALISE conferences will focus on themes that address common interests such as information policy and community engagement.

Potential Opportunities and Strategies

Three "big ideas" for new collaborative projects emerged from the meeting, which participants agreed to pursue, along with other interested partners to be identified:

(1) A workshop to bring together LIS professionals and representatives of innovative collaborative projects to discuss the potential of curricular convergence and resource sharing for the education of library, museum and archives professionals;

(2) Summer institutes to enable LIS programs to invite visiting faculty to offer courses on particular topics to broaden opportunities for both students and LIS faculty; and

(3) Development of an open repository with learning objects for LIS education.

REFERENCES

Association of Indian Universities. (2003). Handbook on Library and Information Science. New Delhi: Association of Indian Universities.

Baba, Abdul Majid. (1999). Accrediting agencies for library and information science education. *Paper presented at the 45th All India Library Association Conference*, New Delhi: UGC

Deshpande, Sunil Gangadhar and Ashtikar, Rajeev. (2005, November). SWOT analysis of distance education for testing its suitability to impart technical and vocational education. *Paper presented at ICDE International Conference*, New Delhi.

Distance education. (n.d.). Retrieved from United States Distance Learning Association website, http://wn.com/United_States_Distance_Learning_Association

Dutta, Bidyarthi and Das, Anup Kumar. (2001). Higher Education in Library and Information Science in India. *ILA Bulletin*. 37(1).

Halder, Sambhu Nath. (2009). Multimodal roles of library and information science professionals in present era. *International Journal of Library and Information Science (IJLIS)*, 1(6), 092-099. Retrieved from *http://www.academicjournals.org/ijlis/pdf/pdf2009/nov/halder.pdf*

Halder, Sambhu Nath. (2012). Library and Information Science Education in India under Open and Distance Mode: A SWOT Analysis. *International Journal of Information Research*. 1(3). pp. 50-59.

Haridasan, Sudharma. (2003). LIS education: Accreditation and its prospects. *ILA Bulletin*, 39 (1), pp.8-10.

Institute of Museum and Library Services. (2007). Trends in Library and Information Science Education: Report of a Meeting. Retrieved from *http://chips.ci.fsu.edu/lis_trends.pdf*

Jana, Sibsankar. (2006). Medium of Instruction in LIS Education in India—Regional Language or English? Analysis through System Approach. *SRELS Journal of Information Management.* 43 (3), pp. 307-18.

Kumar, P S G. (1998). Doctoral studies in Library and Information Science in India: A critical study. *DESIDOC Bulletin of Information Technology.* 18 (1). (pp. 5-8).

Mahapatra, G. (2006). LIS education in India: Emerging paradigms, challenges, and propositions in the digital era. *Presented at the Asia-Pacific Conference on Library & Information Education & Practice.* Singapore.

Mangla, P. B. (1998). Library and Information Science Education: Trends and issues, In Jain, M K, ed. *Fifty years of Library and Information Services in India.* New Delhi: Shipra: 285-293.

Patel, Jashu and Krishan Kumar. (2001). Libraries and Librarianship in India. London: Greenwood Press.

Ramesha and Asundi, A.Y. (2011). Online and virtual learning in LIS education: Changing teaching paradigms. *ISST Journal of Advances in Librarianship*, 2 (1).

Ranganathan, S.R. (1965). Report of the Library Committee of the University Grants.

Reitz, Joan M. (2004). Online Dictionary for Library and Information Science. Retrieved from *http://www.abc-clio.com/ODLIS/searchODLIS.aspx*

Reitz, Joan M. (2008). Online Dictionary for Library and Information Science. Retrieved from *http://lu.com/odlis/index.htm*

Roegge, Kathy. (2007). Trends in Library and Information Science Education Programs. *Metropolitan Library System.* Retrieved from *http://www.mls.lib.il.us/ennounce/2009/03_11/trends.asp*

Roegge, Kathy. (2009). Trends in Library and Information Science Education Programs. Retrieved from *http://www.mls.lib.il.us/ennounce/2009/03_11/trends.asp*

Sacchanand, Chutima. (1998, August). Distance Education in Library and Information Science in Asia and the Pacific Region. *Paper presented at 64th IFLA General Conference*, Amsterdam, Netherlands.

Sarkhel, J. K. (2006, April). Quality assurance and accreditation of LIS education in Indian Universities: Issues and perspectives. In C. Khoo, D. Singh & A.S. Chaudhry (Eds.), *Proceedings of the Asia-Pacific Conference on Library & Information Education & Practice* (pp. 427-431). Singapore: Nanyang Technological University. Retrieved from *http://arizona.openrepository.com/arizona/bitstream/10150/106273/1/ 61.Juran_Krishna_Sarkhel_pp427-431_.pdf*

Satija, M. P. (1998). Whom do we serve? : Doctoral research in Library and

Information Science in India. Desidoc Bulletin of Information Technology, 18(1), pp 19-24.

Satija, M.P. (1993). Research in Librarianship before and after Ranganathan, In. Navalani, K and Satija, M.P, eds. Pettits petals: A tribute to S R Ranganathan. New Delhi: ABC Publishing House: 27-45.

Singh, Joginder, Shahid, Syed Mohd. (2010). Changing Needs of Library and Information Science Curricula in India. *Library Philosophy and Practice.* Retrieved from *http://www.webpages.uidaho.edu/~mbolin/jogindersingh-shahid.htm*

Singh, S. P. (2003). Are we really ready to face challenges of the LIS profession? Papers presented at the 24th All India Conference of IASLIC. Calcutta: IASLIC, (pp.449-456).

Singh, S.P. (2003). Library and information science education in India: Issues and trends. *Malaysian Journal of Library & Information Science*, 8(2). Pp.1-17.

University Grants Commission, India. (1965). Review Committee Report on Library Science in Indian Universities (Chairman: S R Ranganathan). New Delhi: University Grants Commission.

University Grants Commission, India. (1992). Report of the Curriculum Development Committee (CDC) on Library and Information Science (Chairman: P N Kaula). New Delhi: University Grants Commission.

University Grants Commission, India. (2001). UGC model curriculum: Library and Information Science. (Chairman: C R Karisiddappa). New Delhi: University Grants Commission.

Wikipedia : the free encyclopedia. (2011). SWOT Analysis. Retrieved from *http://en.wikipedia.org/wiki/SWOT_analysis*

3

Roles of LIS Professionals

A **librarian** is a person in charge of a library, and is usually trained in librarianship (known either as library science or library and information science). Traditionally, a librarian is associated with collections of books, as demonstrated by the etymology of the word "librarian" (< Latin *liber*, 'book'). The role of a librarian is continuously evolving to meet social and technological needs. However, a modern librarian may deal with information in many formats, including books, magazines, newspapers, audio recordings (both musical and spoken-word), video recordings, maps, manuscripts, photographs and other graphic material, bibliographic databases, web searching, and digital resources. A librarian may provide other information services, including computer provision and training, coordination of public programs, basic literacy education, and assistive equipment for people with disabilities, and help with finding and using community resources (Wikipaedia, 2012).

Presently, librarians are playing an integrated role beyond their traditional job. In a fast changing world, there are new demands and influences on libraries and information centers. Using modern technologies, libraries all over the world are now shifting their emphasis from traditional to multidimensional work force. As a corollary to this, LIS professionals are supposed to play versatile role in different areas of libraries and information centers to meet the expectations and needs of the present situation.

3.1. AS ADVOCATE

LIS professionals act as lawyer when they deal with the issue relating to law such as copyright law, intellectual property right, etc. Librarian champion the cause of academic libraries through various advocacy programs to promote the library and resources. They can communicate news about the library through newsletters, web sites and memos to parents and staff. Their job is to keep principals and teachers up to date on what is happening in the library and to promote library activities and special projects. Schools are learning communities, encompassing students, teachers, administrators and parents (Baule, 1999). Librarians must communicate the mission, goals and objectives of the resource centre to the entire user community (Scheirer, 2000).

3.2. AS CONSORTIA MANAGER

The LIS professionals are responsible for coordinating and overseeing consortium operations, including strategic planning, systems development and project management. Related responsibilities include facilitating communication among the participating libraries. In addition to these responsibilities, the Librarian for consortium operations acts as the consortium's representative with vendors for contracted products and services.

3.3. AS CONSULTANT

Generally speaking, consultants do not provide clients with existing published information, rather they advise to solve problems. The library and information professional often acts as an adviser who recommends both the best sources of information and ways in which to access information. This is a consultancy role which deserves recognition. Scattering of information is hindrance experienced by the users. These necessitates the organization of information sources in a proper way that facilitates easy access to the users. However to be convincing, skills need to be developed to a higher level in order to achieve the librarian as consultant role.

3.4. AS CONTENT MANAGER

The information science world has witnessed a major transformation in the content it has been dealing with. Digital and virtual libraries are a natural outcome of the movement of digitization and inter-networking. Library and documentation centres have increasingly used the technologies of intranets, extranets and portals for specialized techniques of content management and deployment. This information has been put to distinct business advantage by using the techniques of data warehousing, data mining, taxonomies, ontology and industry-specific knowledge maps. Use of Info maps and knowledge mapping are additional competencies for creating visuals for knowledge maps, which makes search and retrieval much easier and enjoyable. Available visualization technologies need to be employed for this purpose.

3.5. AS FACILITATOR

Rapid growth of electronic documents and their availability in the web now creates exploration of information. Even so many printed versions of books, journals have shifted their platform to Internet, which includes freely available and paid publications also. At the same time it is becoming very hard to locate necessary information within least possible time. In these circumstances, librarians are trying to acquire knowledge of different systems and software to manage the sea of information.

Side by side s/he also gains a wide range of proficiency to effectively guide and train the information seekers in their usage. The role of the facilitator if characterized by qualifications would be closely related to the ones of the librarian. It is likely to emerge that the traditional intermediary function of the librarian by its nature could create a basis for the role of the facilitator in a networked community (Schreiber and Moring, 1997). This is the changing role of traditional librarian to ensure that user and/or staff knows how to access relevant sources of information. LIS professionals have not only to deal with greater quantities of information than earlier, but using ICT, have also to change their role from passive providers of information support to more proactive providers of information itself (Rao and Babu, 2001).

The availability of electronic documents on Internet and the support extended by World Wide Web to access these documents have recently increased tremendously. Several print journals have shifted their platform to Web, which includes free and paid publications. In this scenario, it is imperative for the traditional librarian to acquire necessary skills in effective use of modern gadgets and associated software to locate and retrieve the widely dispersed information in the cyberspace. Not only he has to acquaint himself but also gain a degree of proficiency to effectively guide and train the information seekers in their usage. Thus, the traditional librarian has to play the role of facilitator in identification, gathering and arranging information infrastructure such as network access, software access, licenses and passwords to use charged resources like FirstSearch, UnCover, Ovid, etc. The role of the facilitator if characterized by qualifications would be closely related to the ones of the librarian. It is likely to emerge that the traditional intermediary function of the librarian by its nature could create a basis for the role of the facilitator in a networked community (Schreiber and Moring, 1997). Normally, the facilitator does not solve the total information problems of users. He addresses the communications and information needs of the users in one way or another and makes an identification of resources for fulfilling the needs of users.

3.6. AS GUIDE/TEACHER/ EDUCATOR/ TRAINER

Most often LIS professionals acts as a teacher to ensure that patron know how to access relevant sources of information. The shifted role of the teacher-librarian has evolved from "keeper of the books" to "information resource specialist." Teacher-librarians play a vital role in educating users to become information managers and lifetime learners. A big number of users need to be assisted to use the journal literature and different reference tools, like Chemical Abstracts, thesauri, etc. On the other hand, in the Internet era use of e-journals, OPAC and advance search option in using Search Engine, e.g. use of Boolean operators are also needed to be instructed. Present day librarians have a big hand to assist user as and when required. Like classroom teaching, librarians can provide guidance to their user community with Information literacy programme. Information literacy is the ability to access and evaluate information that promotes both independent learning and social responsibility. It is the teacher-librarian's job to show users how to analyze information critically and use it wisely. Users must know how to plan, locate and retrieve information. They process what they find to create a product and the final step is evaluation (Lighthall, 1990).

There are many forms of user education from library tour to bibliographic instruction. Many of those programs are now working with or evolving into information literacy programs with emphasis on the Internet instruction (Martin, 1997). Information literacy education, beyond embracing the basic abilities of reading and writing, now embodies the general ability to understand and perform functions successfully. The term is often paired with areas such as media, computers, culture and information. The goal of information literacy is to ensure that people understand how to, and why they need to, learn about sources in the information society. Some of these sources will be in the library; others will be in the world at large. The definitions of information literacy varies slightly from source to source, though the focus is helping users gain a broad understanding of information sources and enhancing their ability to deal with that information.

To be information literate, an individual must recognize when information is needed and have the ability to locate, evaluate and use effectively the information needed (American Library Association, 1989). There is a growing recognition of the need to train users in information literacy skills. Libraries should take on the role of imparting information literacy skills. For example, The Digital Information Literacy program at The University of Texas at Austin is dedicated to promoting electronic resources to the library users and encourages users to examine the Internet information (Martin, 1997). Three steps in user education end user training is an evolving area of research. Learning to use a library was once a fairly simple activity for the user. Library searching was relatively straight forward, and the end-product easily retrievable. Users are becoming more independent and effective search engines are coming into being. Access to information is not enough and librarians will be encouraged to become editors and create filters to help users select what they want.

- Identify what librarians need to impart to users. The mission of user education aims to help users at all levels learn how to identify the information they need from the morass of information in electronic and other forms.
- Recognize that learning to search is a progressive process Users will have rudimentary skills in their first weeks of training. What should be kept in mind is that they will need help every time they use a library, search the Internet or databases even later.
- Have an important part in playing extension support to users

People go in for do-it-yourself activities. That is true with information seeking. Librarians may prepare users to deal with the complexity of information environment and encourage users to search what they need on their own given the availability of technological support.

3.7. AS INTERMEDIARY

Librarian is a person who functions between the end-user and an online bibliographic retrieval system to assist in database selection, establish telecommunication connections, formulate useful queries in correct syntax and evaluate the relevance of information retrieved. Mediated searching is provided on request in most academic libraries by a public service librarian specially trained in online searching.

An Intermediary is defined by Peter Ingwersen (1992) as "a person or mechanism placed physically between IR (Information Retrieval) systems and actual user with the purpose to transform interactively requests for information to query formulations that suit the retrieval components of one or several IR systems, to model and support the actual user as to his information need and underlying goals and to provide information of potential value to that user from IR systems". Traditionally a human intermediary is a librarian or an information specialist. An IR system includes textpresentations, classification and indexing systems and IR techniques in catalogues and databases or other information sources. However, research in this field is directed towards implementing non-human intermediary functions into online IR systems through user interfaces and system setting. In addition to more efficient and more effective searches by librarians, research has determined that a single librarian or information professional can save the equivalent amount of time of three, or four, or even five end-users. In other words librarians are three, or four, or five times more efficient and more effective than end-users are at performing their own information searching activities (Rao and Babu, 2001). A new note of librarians is to move out at the intermediary position for end user.

In an organization, though librarians began training end-users to perform their own searches, the demand for searches by information professionals have not decreased. End-users having been trained and having performed some of their own searches became aware of the complexities of searching, the limitations of some of the resources and of the searching process especially on World Wide Web. So, a more educated user who continues to perform simple searches on his own behalf, returns to the librarian or information specialist to perform the more complex searches. The effect on librarians has been an increase in workload because the searches are more complex and the amount of time per search has increased. Hence, there will always be a role for the search intermediary. This, probably, is the most important point to remember, because it is why librarians will continue to play a role in the newly emerging digital information world. So, those searches which are not straightforward will always tend to be delegated to an intermediary for querying and providing packaged answer, drawing on a range of resources like print, online bibliographic databases, Internet and Web documents. In India, the availability of infrastructure for exploiting the Web fully like high speed Internet connectivity, access to CDROM databases are in the process of catching up with the advanced countries like USA. However, the lack of the same is not a damper to the enthusiast of young library & information science professionals in the making. They have the idea and vision of what the Web can do and means to them (Rao and Babu, 2001).

3.8. AS KNOWLEDGE MANAGER

The concept and name—"Knowledge Management"—was started and popularized in the business world during the last decade of the 20th century. It was the business world that first recognizes the importance of knowledge in the "global economy" of the "knowledge age". In the new knowledge economy, the possession of relevant and strategic knowledge and its unceasing renewal enables businesses to gain competitive advantage. The applications of knowledge management have now spread to other organizations including government agencies, research and development departments, universities, and others.

The management of information has long been regarded as the domain of librarians and libraries. Librarians and information professionals are trained to be experts in information searching, selecting, acquiring, organizing, preserving, repackaging, disseminating, and serving. However, professionals in information technology and systems have also regarded information management as their domain because of the recent advances in information technology and systems which drive and underpin information management. One of the clearest evidences of this is that the positions of "Chief Information Officer" (CIO) in many organizations are generally held by information technologists instead of librarians. In fact, most of the work of CIOs has to do with developing and managing the IT infrastructure and systems, not the managing of information per se.

With the growing interest in knowledge management, many questions have been raised in the minds of librarians regarding: the difference between information and knowledge; between information management and knowledge management; who should be in charge of information and knowledge management; would librarians and information professionals with appropriate education and training in library and information science be most suitable for the position of "Chief Knowledge Officer" (CKO) in their organizations; and what libraries can do in implementing knowledge management.

Knowledge Management (KM) involves the identification and analysis of available and required knowledge and the subsequent planning and control of actions to develop knowledge assets so as to fulfill organizational objectives.

Librarians play a major role in transforming data into information, and information into knowledge management. They accomplish this through a number of steps such as acquiring, organizing and indexing information, in addition to helping the searchers in evaluating and critically appraising the information retrieved and gathered.

LIS professionals have been playing a vital role in Knowledge Management and, if anything, serves to 'stake a claim' in Knowledge Management territory, in part, as a vehicle for enhancing the professional image and role or the information professional.

Librarians in general and Documentation and Information Center's (DIC) librarians and information professionals in particular, do believe that their role in information management combined with their knowledge of the user is really Knowledge Management, librarians and information professionals have been involved for years, in KM within libraries and information centers, but now is the time to be more involved in the other institution strategies and plans. Librarians will grasp the opportunity to develop a fully integrated virtual and physical knowledge base both at specific easily accessible geographical locations and directly to the desktop via the Net.

Librarian as a part of KM system can effectively participate in the process of knowledge creation which includes mechanisms for knowledge capture, exploitation and protection besides in required infrastructure creation by the virtue of capabilities gained as Information Managers of the organization Librarians, in future, would move from the background to the center of the organization. They would shed their traditional role as a part of support group, uninvolved in any critical functions, to a prominent position to jointly hold the reins of knowledge management with users and the technology experts. They would help steer and shape the knowledge policies, structures, processes, and systems that will nurture organizational learning (Rao and Babu, 2001).

Some of the qualities of a librarian to become a knowledge manager:

(a) Providing services to the user community.

(b) Sharing the information and understanding the user needs.

(c) Theoretical and practical experience in designing and implementing information systems.

(d) Analyzing the documents, classifying and storing them for easy retrieval.

(e) Knowledge of current advances in information systems and technologies and their application in libraries.

(f) Building the index, using standard vocabulary.

(g) Ability to effectively teach end-users, individually and in groups.

Knowledge Management (KM) involves the identification and analysis of available and required knowledge, and the subsequent planning and control of actions to develop knowledge assets so as to fulfill organizational objectives. Organizations worldwide are realizing the advantages of enlisting librarians in the KM systems. Librarian as a part of KM system can effectively participate in the process of knowledge creation which includes mechanisms for knowledge capture, exploitation and protection besides in required infrastructure creation by the virtue of capabilities gained as Information Managers of the organization. The creation of the knowledge center in an organization normally involves contributions from three groups of experts such as users, knowledge professionals and technology experts. Knowledge professionals are the individuals in the knowledge center who have the skills, training and know-how to organize knowledge into systems and structures that facilitate the productive use of knowledge resources. They include librarians, managers, archivists, and others. Librarians to become Knowledge Managers or Professionals should possess variety of talents and perform the work with high level skill and expertise. They should be able to extract, filter and disseminate vital external knowledge, and work side by side with users in collecting and analyzing strategic intelligence throughout the organization. Librarians, in future, would move from the background to the center of the organization. They would shed their traditional role as a part of support group, uninvolved in any critical functions, to a prominent position to jointly hold the reins of knowledge management with users and the technology experts. They would help steer and shape the knowledge policies, structures, processes, and systems that will nurture organizational learning (Seonghee, 1999).

3.9. AS RESEARCHER

LIS professionals have played a crucial role in research process. They are highly skilled in the research process and possess a unique knowledge of both the breadth and depth of information resources in various subject specialties.

Their active participation in research teams are very much important to critical analysis. By facilitating access to nascent information in the way to finding it, analyzing, synthesizing and packaging the LIS professionals would move to the beginning of the information production cycle, playing a more substantial role in the information creation process. Teams within an organization should have an information professional who is responsible for the information gathering skills of the team (Rao and Babu, 2001). To fulfill research work in least possible time the help of LIS professionals is inescapable. They are always happy to help by providing organized information in right time on the basis of research scholar's demand.

Librarians are highly skilled in the research process and possess a unique knowledge of the breadth and depth of information resources in various subject specialties. Librarians are increasingly going to participate in and be critical members of research teams. By facilitating access to information – finding it, analyzing, synthesizing, and packaging - librarians would move to the beginning of the information production cycle, playing a more substantial role in the information creation process. Teams within an organization should have an information professional who is responsible for the information gathering skills of the team.

3.10. AS SIFTER

The term sifter is well known in the field of computer science. Actually sifter or siftware is nothing but, it is "software programs to extract unknown, valid and actionable patterns, associations, changes, anomalies and rules from large databases". This process is also known as "Data Mining". The Internet and Web provide access to vast information resources. The term "sifter" may be used for the skilled librarian who helps users make sense and order of the resources. The future belongs neither to the conduit or content players but to those who control the filtering, searching and sense-making tools to navigate through the expanses of cyberspace. In other words, the librarian can be a key player in the emerging scenario (Rao and Babu, 2001).

3.11. AS WEB DESIGNER FOR LIBRARY PORTAL

The use rate of Internet is increasing at a galloping stride. The Internet can now be accessed almost anywhere by numerous means and thus the recent trends is to allowing users to connect to the Internet not only from the library but from the remote places.

A well viewed interface always attracts the users and increasingly relevant to the way people access and use digital technologies. A beneficial way for librarians to break out of their insularity is to become much more closely involved and collaborate in the work of computer and information scientists in tasks such as design, organization, development and maintenance of digital library repositories, interfaces, search engines, networks and web documents (Rao and Babu, 2001).

As educators who organize and evaluate information resources, academic librarians bring unique perspectives and skills to the development of portals in their colleges and universities to campus portal planning and implementation, they bring their expertise with content, their knowledge of copyright, their commitment to customer service, and their experience in creating customized web-based information delivery systems.

- **Content** : Academic librarians provide credible content that has been selected for a specific learning community. Their library's homepages and collections have what every web site wants: brand and content. Libraries have the brand name of the academic institution they serve and content that has been customized to meet the needs of their users. To students who may have difficulty determining what is valuable and what is useless on the web, the library offers a safe harbor in a flood of information. Increasingly the content of libraries is in digital form and is composed of databases. Click on any library homepage and you will find an array of databases selected to support the academic programs offered by the institution. These databases are made available both on and off campus through licenses arranged through the library.
- **Copyright** : Librarian's knowledge of current copyright policy is being called upon now more than ever in setting up electronic reserves and online information for learning portals created using blackboard and other web-based course management systems. Faculty members and students may assume that if educational material is on the web, no copyright restrictions apply. However, this is true only if the copyright for the work has expired, its author has allowed the work to go into the public domain, or the work was authored by the federal government. Since there is a mix of works in the public domain

and under copyright on the internet and some works under copyright are posted without authorization, it is not always clear which are in the public domain. Librarians provide guidance in determining which web-based materials are under copyright and seek permission for use of these works with the copyright clearance center and other agencies. Librarians inform faculty about the fair use guidelines.

- **Customer Service :** As libraries make more digital resources available on the web, research is increasingly conducted outside the physical library. However, remote users want interactive assistance from a qualified human being and not just a help button to click on. Librarians have developed a number of ways to extend person-to-person reference service in a digital environment that are applicable in supporting portal use on campus. Digital Reference Services (DRS) offer quality service at any time to users outside the library. DRS refer to all internet-based, human-mediated information services, including those based in library settings and other types of organizations. Such services range from e-mail reference which libraries have offered for years, to online reference chat which many librarians are now implementing.

3.12. AS DETECTOR AND INSTRUCTOR OF PLAGIARISM

The proliferation of student plagiarism on university campuses is paralleled by the increasing number of articles appearing in academic journals presenting varying opinions on the topic. Opinions run the gamut from outrage at the student offenders to pointing fingers at faculty members who fail to create plagiarism-proof assignments. One also reads about controversial new methods for deterring and detecting plagiarism, most notably, online plagiarism detection systems. In surveying the literature, one can construct valid arguments for each point of view. The plagiarism dilemma from a librarian's vantage point, and will outline the strong support that has been offered to teaching faculty with plagiarism problems by the Joan and Donald E. Axinn Library of Hofstra University. It will also examine how Hofstra

University decided to subscribe to Turnítin.com (www.turnitin.com), a popular but controversial online plagiarism detection system.

Brandt (2002) gives five basic things librarians can do during to prevent plagiarism:

- **Define it.** Clarify what it is. Describe its variations. Discuss how it happens.
- **Show examples to make it clear.** Demonstrate what someone should or shouldn't do. Points to sites that can help them avoid it.
- **Describe its consequences.** Help students understand what can happen in terms they will relate to promote it, or rather, promote its prevention. Display messages in the library, mention it on website, talk about it.
- **Discuss it.** Don't be passive. Devote some time to it in every lecture or class you give.

To accomplish these kinds of goals, instructional sessions and online tutorials with selfgrading quizzes have been developed by many institutions with varying degrees of success. Harvard Graduate School of Education developed the highly successful tutorial "APA exposed: everything you always wanted to know about APA format but were afraid to ask" (Mages and Garson, 2010). However, the School of Health and Sciences at the University of Liverpool found considerably less success with their online tool containing referencing and anti-plagiarism multimedia lectures (Brown, Dickson, Humphreys, McQuillan, and Smears, 2008). Park, Mardis, and Ury (2011) were very successful with their approach taken at Northwest Missouri State Unversity's B.D. Owens Library which is described as a "four-pillared approach to teach students about the intricacies of citation: textbooks (e.g style manuals), tutorials (e.g. online tutorials, citation assistance, and general plagiarism prevention techniques), instruction (e.g. information literacy instruction), and reference (e.g. individual help with citing)".

3.13. AS INFORMATION FILTERER

Special librarians, in the role of information filter, have traditionally relied on qualities such as "tact, patience, persistence" and on "knowledge of one's town". Only by cultivating a thorough understanding of their organization and their organizational clients' information needs and preferences could librarians hope to serve as effective information intermediaries (Jester, 1992). But we have entered the age of the "virtual library," an age in which desktop Personal Computers and end-user-targeted electronic reference products allow library clients to access electronic information remotely and thus serve - in theory, at least - as their own information filters. Does that mean that the computer is serving the special librarian's role? Bank of Montreal Business Information Centre Manager Sylvia E.A. Piggott, in discussing the bank's virtual-library project, offers a definitive answer: "Until such time as computers are capable of matching human intelligence, and ... all the information required by a user is delivered at his/her desktop at an affordable price, the role of the librarian in the process of managing and imparting knowledge will remain central" (Piggott, 1993).

That does not mean, that the librarian's role is not changing. One lesson from the Bank of Montreal's experience is that, while librarians retain an information filtering role, the manner in which they fulfill that role is changing dramatically. Rather than to gather, filter and deliver information, the bank's librarians have become skilled at "selecting, evaluating, and implementing ... electronic information sources". In other words, in the virtual library, the librarian filters information primarily by judiciously selecting and implementing electronic tools.

3.14. AS INTELLIGENT AGENTS

The rapid growth of unstructured data on Internet and World Wide Web has created significant problems related to the efficiency and accuracy of information retrieval. In addition, information repositories on Internet are heterogeneous, inconsistent and sometimes incomplete (Bowman et al., 1994). To make effective use of this wealth of information, a number of resource discovery tools have been created. In Internet browsing, the user follows the hypertext links to locate the information. When the size of the Web increased beyond few sites and a small number of documents it became clear that manual browsing through a significant portion of the hypertext structure is no longer possible (Koster, 1995). To solve this problem and locate information required by the user search engines have been developed. Many of the search engines use the concept of a 'robot' or 'spider', an automated browsing program. A web robot is a piece of program that traverses the Web's hypertext structure by retrieving a document and recursively retrieving all documents that are referenced and develops huge index database. When a user performs a search on a topic or keyword, Web search engines returns several thousands of hits, many of which may not be relevant to the user's enquiry. The size and wide coverage of such a database can make it difficult to quickly and effectively track down relevant information using the limited searching features that are available (Stanley, 1997). In order to provide a solution

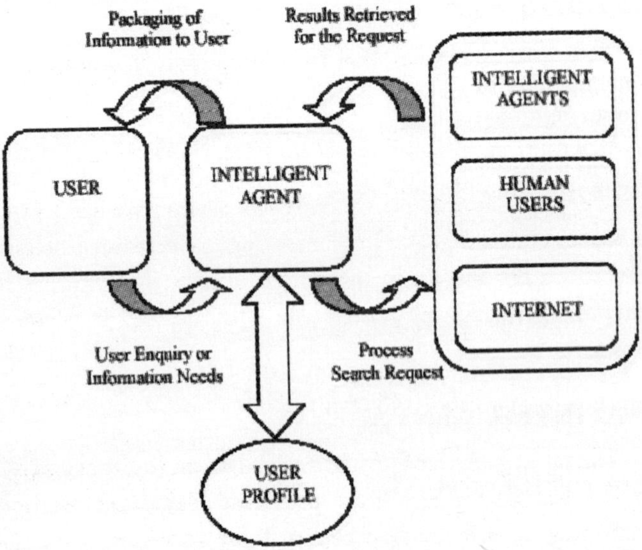

Working of Intelligent Agents

to this problem, Intelligent Agents have been developed. Intelligent Agents are autonomous and adaptive computer programs operating within software environments such as operating systems, databases, or computer networks. Intelligent Agent technology combines artificial intelligence (reasoning, planning, natural language processing, etc), and system development techniques (object-oriented programming, scripting languages, human-machine interfaces, distributed processing, etc) to produce a new generation of software that can, based on user preferences, perform routine tasks for users (Meek, 1995). Although they are still in their infancy, the Intelligent Agents of tomorrow have the promise to relieve users of the time-consuming and tedious searches through a massive, intricate and globally dispersed Web of electronic information. These agents will find, assemble and analyze information that users need to solve problems, become better informed and make intelligent decisions (Roesler and Hawjins, 1994). Librarians have been efficiently accomplishing many of the tasks at which the artificial intelligence community is now working to make software agents competent. Therefore, the software agents can be developed by a look at how human information agents carryout their work (Zick, 2000). Intelligent Agents will accelerate the change in the librarian's role, enabling more complex tasks like gathering a portfolio of information on particular topic to be done electronically. This need not be construed as a threat, for; it is also an opportunity to relieve the librarian of the drudgework of searching for information, which more often than not is a boring task. If machines can do this work, librarians can spend their time on more interesting tasks (Library Association, 1997).

Librarian Vis-a-Vis Intelligent Agents

Will the librarian exists in the Internet environment due to proliferation of Intelligent Agents? What roles the librarians are going to play? Librarians are becoming more important in the information-centric universe. Intelligent Agents will act as catalysts to enhance the role of librarians. Librarians are already fulfilling new roles as content providers, search strategists, digital catalogers and information mechanics. These roles will only grow and new opportunities will flourish with the development of truly intelligent agents that build upon the experience of librarians and information professionals (Valauskas, 1997). The precise information needs of a user/person can be grasped quickly and correctly by another human being. To convert the information needs or queries into a machine-readable and executable form often is very involved and time consuming. Yet the full essence of the user needs may remain un-captured in this process. The adequacy, appropriateness, and timeliness of the information gathered by Intelligent Agents can be judged best either by the librarian or the user of the information. In the event of non-availability of the user for consultation librarian is the best judge. The creator of Intelligent Agents utilizes the abilities that are available in artificial intelligence, computer hardware, software, communication and databases technologies, etc. to mimic the task of the librarians explained above.

3.15. AS END-USERS' TRAINER / EDUCATOR

The number and variety of information sources available, whether locally or remotely via the www have increased greatly, and users in many cases have not been able to keep up with all of the choices open to them. Few users of the libraries are effective and efficient in accessing information resources. However, no matter how sophisticated interfaces and search engines come up in future information access systems, people still would need to be educated regarding their usage. Users will need to possess an understanding of essential information gathering skills and tools. The areas in which training is given by the librarian would include not only the use of electronic primary journals from many different publishers, but also the use of abstracts and indexing databases, databanks, CD-ROM publications and document delivery services. End-user training aspect of librarian would also include organization of information resources, search strategies, tools, information searching skills, awareness of resource constraints and alerts to users on new resources in their subject area. The librarian therefore, has a critical role in the digital library of future as educator or end-user trainer.

3.16. AS WEB SITE BUILDER OR PUBLISHER

The traditional skill of a librarian in locating, evaluating and organizing the information would be of immense use in the creation, development and content filling of a web site for the organization and library. Web site of an organization provides access to external resources, where web pages specific to their discipline are available. Managing organization's own information on the web site includes details of course information, directories, statutes, annual reports, etc., The role of the librarian while creating a web page is to deliver information about the library and its services like hours of service, location of services, details of library staff, library policies, an interface to the library Online Public Access Catalog (OPAC), etc.

3.17. AS INTERFACE DESIGNER

Interface design is going to become increasingly important and increasingly relevant to the way people access and use digital technologies. A beneficial way for librarians to break out of their insularity is to become much more closely involved and collaborate in the work of computer and information scientists in tasks such as design, organization, development, and maintenance of digital library repositories, interfaces, search engines, networks and web documents. Librarian can help in the design of technology-based information services and share their intimate knowledge of what users want and need as they have years of experience in helping patrons utilize electronic media and subsequently using Internet and World Wide Web.

3.18. AS BIBLIO-THERAPIST / INFORMATION THERAPIST

'Information Therapy is the prescription of the right information, to the right person, at the right time to help make a better health decision.' This simple definition of Information Therapy raises many questions. How can information have therapeutic effects? What do we mean by 'the right information'? Isn't every person who needs health information a 'right person'? And is there a 'right time' to provide health information? Isn't now as good as any time?

This is a guest post by Vasumathi Sriganesh, CEO, QMed Knowledge Foundation, Mumbai, when Mr and Mrs Shukla's child was diagnosed with 'Down's syndrome', they wanted all possible information on the illness. Endless hours of searching on Google provided little useful information, driving them to frustration. On a friend's advice, they visited a consumer health library. There, a helpful and informed librarian scanned through the catalog and gave them a list of popular books on the subject, many of which were written by parents of children of Down's syndrome. In today's high-tech age, visiting a library was the Shuklas' last resort. However, it clearly ended up being the best one.

Health-related information is useful if it is available to people in the right doses at the right time, but only if it is authentic and beneficial. The problem is that very often – and alarmingly so – the information people get is inaccurate. In such cases, the information can be actually harmful, rather than being helpful. It may be the result of wrong research. It maybe outdated. It may be too complicated for people to understand. It may not be available unless people are ready to pay a substantial fee. And sometimes we simply do not get information because our healthcare providers forget to tell us some facts or instructions. This could happen due to human factors like their overly busy schedule, or they may assume that we already know these facts.

A simple example illustrates this: A lady went to have a blood sugar test. A lab technician drew her blood when she was on an empty stomach. She was then told to eat and come after two hours. She went home, ate after an hour and came back within two hours of her first visit to the lab. A clearer instruction would have been, 'Come back to give a sample two hours after you have eaten.' For the technician, this was routine knowledge. Without realizing this, he had assumed that anyone who came for this test would know these facts. A simple handout for such patients would have made a big difference. In this case, luckily the patient herself had a doubt and gave the second blood sample after another hour.

3.19. AS CHANGE AGENTS FOR INSTITUTIONAL REPOSITORIES

In the search for relevant literature on the roles of librarians in the setting up of institutional repositories, the following themes emerged:

(a) **Collection management and stewardship of collection:** Literature indicates that librarians have a critical position in the collection management and preservation through institutional repositories. Librarians have the capability to add authors or give permission to authors to self archive materials in the repository (Crow 2002; Harnad 2001; Lynch 2003). Librarians upgrade their knowledge synchronously with information environment and can adapt themselves with their new roles as a collection administrator of digital materials (Branin et al., 2000; Lee 2000; Pettijohn and Neville 2003). Literature also indicates that librarians are facing problems in collection management because the acquisition of collections is in the hands of faculties (Allard et al., 2005). To settle the contents of institutional repository, students and faculties as authors should be involved with self archiving to submit their works to institutional repository (Barton et al., 2003; Bell 2004; Campbell et al., 2004; Cervone 2004; Crow 2002; Gadd et al., 2003; Johnson 2002; Mackie 2004). But, it is crystal clear that after acquisition the collection needs supervision, which should be the responsibility of the librarians. Authors are in charge of selecting items to add to repository and librarians are the stewards of this collection (Genoni 2004) especially for preserving the repository (Wheatley 2004). There is no doubt to entrust this responsibility to librarians since history shows librarians have navigated the way in using and designing new technologies. Librarians are expert in adjustment with new changes and professional in development of the environment (Branin et al., 2000).

(b) **Understanding of software and giving training to authors:** Deciding about the software is the first step in creating an institutional repository and literature shows Kamraninia, K. & Abrizah, A. that librarians have enough knowledge of working with institutional repository software. Allard et al., 2005 contend that librarians should comprehend the software with the intention that they can design repositories in their libraries. They should also have the ability to create institutional repository that is useable by the software extender since authors and their contributions in institutional repository is one of the significant elements in the development of institutional repositories. With a consideration of natural extension of preparation and training of users, librarians should educate authors to deposit their intellectual works to institutional repositories. Education would consist of assisting university community to learn the use of institutional repository software to accomplish self archiving (Abrizah, 2010).

(c) **Establishing a standard metadata and comprehensive catalogue system:** In the past, metadata was defined as a role for librarians but now authors have authorization to submitting metadata. Librarians should establish the clear metadata standards so that authors can use it. The standards can be provided as a set of development guidelines for institutional repository creators. It can help authors to do self archiving with the predicted contents and standard metadata. Abrizah (2010) pointed to the creation of guidelines concerning metadata as a task for librarian. During an effort to provide a complete repository which can cover unique items, librarians should prepare a comprehensive system for cataloging and indexing the materials.

(d) **Review submission for quality of content:** Quality content verification is another essential need for the development of an institutional repository. Because self archiving by authors is an important component of institutional repository, the existence of a group that have the ability to review the quality content of final submissions and check the metadata is necessary. Lynch (2003) believes that the institutional repository environment would be orderly if librarians can be answerable to this role because some institutional repositories do not want to take author's assistance due to the need of quality checks.

(e) **Persuading authors to contribute with self archiving**: Self-submission of material by faculty members need librarians' enthusiasm and in the learning process of self archiving, authors need to be exposed to awareness about copyright issues and become familiar with new technologies. Unfortunately past studies show that faculty members do not carry out self-submission. Swan and Brown (2005) found that the majority of authors were unconscious about the benefits of publishing their works in institutional repository. Their research showed less than one third of the respondents were using OAI search engines to find out their required information through the institutional repository and only 10% of the authors were aware about SHERPA/RoMEO list of publishers' permissions policy with respect to self archiving. Lack of authors' desire in depositing their works in the institutional repository, could be the main reason for the slow growth in the development of institutional repositories. According to McDowell's research, all involved librarians in institutional repository development in Census of Institutional Repositories in the US, reported that they are facing problem in taking on contents from graduate students, faculties and researchers (McDowell, 2007). So, cheering of authors to deposit their intellectual works through self archiving to institutional repository in order to enable development of collection is considered as librarians' task. In some cases self archiving is a tough task for some authors. A study in University of Glasgow shows that submitting outputs of researchers on behalf of those who cannot self archive their materials is another solution to make them contribute (Genoni, 2004).

(f) **Training users search technique in institutional repository:** Librarians as crucial bodies in developing institutional repositories should help users and authors to fill content into the institutional repositories and guide them to extract from institutional repositories. They should teach users that how they can recruit search techniques to use the available resources. Preparing the connections for making materials accessible for users is an opportunity to persuade them to become involved with institutional repositories. Since understanding of user's needs is the base of development of metadata and research tools, building a search interface that makes possible searching and accessing to the materials in institutional repositories, is a duty for reference librarians. Beside this, it facilitates search and increase access to resources and information, bringing the institutional repository contents together in library database or library catalogs. Inclusion of institutional repository content in databases and catalogs will increase the chance of researcher to find their relevant resources (Jenkins et al., 2005).

(g) **Promotion and marketing:** Librarians can provide a team with essential information to promote institutional repository. With recognition of organizations and departments as potential institutional repository communities they can promote and develop their library's repositories. Institutional repository concept may need more explanation, marketing and a multiplicity of concerns by librarians (Jenkins et al., 2005). It is essential that librarians be familiar with the library repository to efficiently promote institutional repositories. Beside, providing good search tools and cataloguing the repository materials will make institutional repository contents more accessible.

3.20. LIBRARIANS' ROLE IN EDUCATIONAL EVALUATION

Despite the criticisms of accreditation that have appeared in the higher education press, such as those leveled by William R. Dill and colleagues, the need for quality assurance in education and professional practice is as strong today as it was a century ago, when the system of accreditation began. Indeed, the technological and social changes now underway emphasize the need for innovative and reliable methods for establishing quality in education and for protecting the public against fraudulent and worthless educational programs. The creation of national standards facilitates professional mobility. Today's workers engage in several career changes involving lifelong learning and professional preparation. Contemporary learners browse and select courses from among a variety of institutions, increasing the importance of having a systematic process of transferring credits. In globalized era, international students seek recognition of educational achievement and reciprocity of professional credentials worldwide. The delivery of instruction in time and location independent modes also challenges the old accreditation structures and calls for new approaches to quality assurance.

Technology has prompted librarians to reconsider the basis and rationale for virtually every traditional process and standard. It is only natural that new models for the evaluation of libraries are needed. The changes in the role, value, and organizational structure of accreditation provide an opportunity for the library community to develop new ways to demonstrate their importance and worth. A first step is to acquire a clear understanding of the goals and process of accreditation and assessment; a second is to establish standards compatible with these goals; and a third is the ability to implement assessment to demonstrate conformity to standards.

The turmoil in the world of accreditation in the early and mid-nineties has stimulated standards revision among almost all accrediting agencies in order to address the criticism that standards are built too much around inputs to educational operations, too little around what students learn and graduates can do. Although there is no accrediting body for libraries independent of the parent institution, library associations frequently have input into standards. Among academic libraries, the Association of College and Research Libraries has for many years proclaimed standards that can be used by accreditation teams to assess libraries. In the recent past these standards have begun to reflect the shift from quantitative, input-based standards to outcomes-based standards. This approach is particularly challenging for librarians, because libraries have typically and traditionally operated on an input model. Nevertheless, academic librarians have engaged the issue and are working to develop new standards and new models for evaluation. The recent ACRL Task Force on Academic Library Outcomes Assessment Report has had demonstrable effect on the Standards for College Libraries. The Standards for University Library Performance and the Standards for Community, Junior, and Technical College Learning Resources Programs, due for revision in 2002 and 2000 respectively, are likely to reflect an even greater commitment to outcomes assessment.

Clearly, librarians can establish standards that are outcome based. Working within the framework of outcomes assessment is not a trivial undertaking. As Ralph Wolff points out, the outcomes model called for by accreditation, has the potential to "transform" the library. He cites four organizing principles—resources, research, students, and learning—around which to create an assessment model for libraries. One of the most well developed examples of outcomes assessment in libraries is the effect of the library on student learning as demonstrated by information literacy. The task of implementing assessment requires an understanding not only of the planning process—articulating a mission and determining goals and objectives—but also a commitment to what is often called "a culture of evidence." Having a working knowledge of such basic evaluation techniques as user surveys, focus groups, interviews, sampling, citation patterns, and bibliometrics is necessary for a library to operate in such a culture. These techniques may be either quantitative or qualitative, but their application must be driven by the mission of the institution itself. They must be examined in terms of reliability (they produce consistent results regardless of who is administering them) and internal validity (they measure what is intended). This requires a skill set that librarians must acquire either at the master's degree or later on, in the workplace. It also requires the ability to make the shift in thinking that is suggested in Wolff's thought-provoking essay.

Librarians can also contribute to the accreditation activities that take place on campus. Librarians who participate in accreditation activities, both in the campus preparation for accreditation and as members of the site visit team, have the opportunity to view the role of the library in the context of the overall institutional mission and goals. Otherwise, they will be perceived as a lobby group whose position is suspect. Librarians can also make a significant contribution at the national level by developing and reporting useful quality indicators. To the extent that the library community can stay in a dialogue with the various sectors in accreditation and higher education, the measures or indicators that are developed will have applicability and recognized strength among the various organizations that support libraries and fund them. In other words, regardless of whether there can be developed a "national gold standard" that everyone recognizes as "the excellent library," a significant accomplishment will have taken place.

Each library, regardless of its location or context or size, can strive toward excellence. While it is unlikely that a specific profile of excellence can be developed, it should be possible to develop a set of indicators by asking questions such as:

- Does the library survey its constituents on a regular basis?
- Does the library examine what proportion of its user base interacts with the library in a given time period?
- Does the library assess the effect of its instructional program on students' learning?
- Does the library monitor and examine users' success in obtaining needed materials?
- Does the library explore users' understanding of the role of the library in their teaching, learning, and research?
- How does the library ensure that students who are part of the learning community have access to appropriate materials at a location remote from the campus?

Since assessment is institution-specific, it is not easy or appropriate to generalize across institutions. Each library must undertake its own assessment process, within the context of its parent institution. A good introduction to library evaluation is F.W. Lancaster's book. "If You Want to Evaluate Your Library." This constitutes one of the major paradigm shifts brought about by the changes within higher education and accreditation. Such steps are essential if librarians are to establish the centrality of the library in the assessment of quality in higher education. The restructuring of the role and responsibility for quality assurance in higher education that took place during the 1990s produced new organizations, new standards, and new processes. Librarians have taken this restructuring as an opportunity to review and revise standards for libraries and to participate in the accreditation process of their parent institutions. This has implications for the ways in which libraries demonstrate their worth and importance to society. New knowledge and skills may be required if academic librarians are to fulfill their role and use this opportunity. In today's environment, accreditation is seen to be the external validation of an internal quality assurance process. This is the challenge that awaits the academic library community.

REFERENCES

Baule, S. (1999). Information power: building partnerships for learning. *Book Report.* 18(3): pp. 42-43.

Burke, Margaret. (2004). Deterring plagiarism: a new role for librarians. *Library Philosophy and Practice.* 6(2). Retrieved from *http://www.webpages.uidaho.edu/~mbolin/burke.pdf*

Casey, M. E. Savastinuk, L. C. (2006). Library 2.0: service for the next generation library. *Library Journal.* Retrieved from *http://www.libraryjournal.com/article/CA6365200.html*

Castelli, D. (2006). Digital libraries of the future and the role of libraries. *Library Hi Tech.* 24(4): 496-503.

Halder, Sambhu Nath. (2009). Multimodal roles of library and information science professionals in present era. *International Journal of Library and Information Science (IJLIS).* 1(6). pp. 092-099. Retrieved from *http://www.academicjournals.org/ijlis*

INDIA. National Knowledge Commission. (2005). Annexure to NKC recommendations on Libraries. Retrieved from *http://knowledgecommission.gov.in/downloads/recommendations/LibrariesAnnex.pdf.*

INDIA. National Knowledge Commission. (2005). NKC recommendations on libraries: letter to the Prime Minister. *http://knowledgecommission.gov.in/downloads/recommendations/LibrariesLetterPM.pdf*

Ingwersen, P. (1992). Information Retrieval Interaction. London: Taylor Graham pp. 228.

Lighthall, L. (1990). Pivotal role of teacher-librarians. The Canadian School Executive,

Murthy, T. A. V., Cholin, V. S., Vijayakumar, J. K. (2005). UGC-INFLIBNET initiatives in e-journal consortia and digital library of doctoral theses for Indian universities. *In proceedings of National Conference on Digital Library and e-Theses (NCDLET)* Kolkata, Jadavpur University. Retrieved from *http://eprints.rclis.org/archive/00005658/01/vijayakumarjk_09.pdf*

Rai, A. S. (2007). Effective utilisation of hybrid library (digital & print media) in engineering colleges in Bangalore: descriptive study. *Indian Journal of Technical Education.* 30(*4*).

Rao, KN, Babu, KH. (2001). Role of librarian in Internet and World Wide Web environment. *Informing Science.* 4 (1). Retrieved from *http://inform.nu/Articles/Vol4/v4n1p025034.pdf*

Rath, P. (2006). Preparing library and information professionals for the 21st century: Issue and challenges for library and information science educators in India. In: Khoo, C.; Singh, D.; Chaudhry, A.S. (Eds.), *Proceedings of the Asia-Pacific Conference on Library & Information Education & Practice (ALIEP 2006),* Singapore, p. 35-40.

Reitz, J. M. (2004). Online Dictionary for Library and Information Science. Retrieved from *http://lu.com/odlis/index.htm*

Scheirer B (2000). The changing role of the teacher-librarian in the twenty-first century Available at *http://www.usask.ca/education/coursework/802papers/scheirer/scheirer.htm*

Schreiber, T, Moring, C. (1997). The Communicative and Organizational Competencies of the Librarian in Networked Learning Support: A Comparative Analysis of the Roles of the Facilitator and the Librarian. In, *2nd International Symposium on Networked Learner Support: New Services, Roles and Partnerships for the On-line Learning Environment.* Sheffield, England. Retrieved from *http://www.netways.shef.ac.uk/rbase/papers/moring.htm*

Sharma, P. L. (2005). Changing role of librarians in digital library era and need of professional skills, efficiency & competency. Retrieved from *https://drtc.isibang.ac.in/handle/1849/407*

Sridhar, M. S. (2004). Skill requirements of library professional in the Electronic Environment of Twenty first century. In Mahapatra, M. and Ramesh, D. B. *Information Technology application in libraries: A text book for beginners* pp. 597-606

Tang, Jinhong. (1998). The expanding roles of librarians for the new millennium. Retrieved from *http://www.iassistdata.org/downloads/iqvol221tang.pdf*

UGC model curriculum (2001). Library & Information Science, UGC, New Delhi.

Wiederhold, G. (1995). Digital Libraries: Value and productivity. Commun. ACM Digital Library. 38(*4*). Retrieved from *http://dl.acm.org/citation.cfm?id=205347*

Wikipedia, the free encyclopedia. (2012). Librarian. Retrieved from *http://en.wikipedia.org/wiki/Librarian*

4

E-literacy & LIS Professionals

The main and foremost aim of LIS professionals is to provide packaged information as and when needed to their user(s). In this regard information should be organized in different form depending on the users need. Information literacy is the process of knowing different aspect of information. But, in the present era a huge number of information sources assume an electronic form, information literacy nowadays includes, *e-literacy* that may be thought of as information literacy in an age of digital information.

In the information horizon with the advent of the web, some former restrictions in the experience of studying – limited information resources, limited access to readymade solutions, and a working environment limited to interaction with tutors and classmates are being removed. As in information systems we rework our transferable skills materials to include a deeper treatment of information and communication, we come into contact with, and are interested in, a more general agenda of information literacy and e-literacy developing in the library and information centers. There are important crossovers and possible conflicts here. New problematic of information and learning may be emerging.

4.1. INFORMATION LITERACY

To be information literate a person must be able to recognize when information is needed and have the ability to locate, evaluate, and use effectively the needed information (American Library Association, 1998). Information Literacy is the ability to make significant connections to form interpretation to evaluate situation, and to provide context.

Information literacy is more than just the routine application of a particular set of operational information skills: it is a way of knowing. Information literate individuals understand and know the context of their information environments and the ways in which information is organized into information caches. The term 'information cache' is introduced here to describe the variety of information types and sources that exist and can be accessed within an information environment. Like the physical environment, information environments have topography of paths, nodes and edges. Hence, an information literate person can navigate the landscape of his or her environment and understands its ecology (Lloyd, 2003).

Information literacy includes 'library research skills and IT literacy' but it is broader than these. Information literacy is not just about finding and presenting information, it is about higher order analysis, synthesis, critical thinking and problem solving. It involves seeking and using information for independent learning, lifelong learning, participative citizenship and social responsibility (Lupton, Glanville, McDonald, Selzer, 2004). The overview of Koltay (2007) information literacy gained an important place in Library and Information Science (LIS) education, information literacy however often includes (predominantly verbal) communication. Information literacy or at least its communicative features should be made a subject of psycholinguistics and cognitive science as information literacy stresses the importance of gaining control over how we interact with information and it consists of processes that are widely unknown thus require cognitive enquiry. It would be however premature to draw consequences of a cognitive enquiry not yet carried out.

4.2. E-LITERACY

Transformation literacy required in the new economy characterized by changes in social, political, economic and civic life that have come in the wake of globalization in the 21st century. New literacy include e-literacy which consists of awareness of the IT and the information environment, confidence in using generic IT and information tools and applications, evaluation of information-handling operations and products, which translates into the ability to access, understand, analyze and critique information and the capacity to produce, communicate and use knowledge from various sources for varied tasks and activities (Martin, Rader, 2003). E-literacy is a crucial enabler of individuals and institutions in moving successfully in a world reliant upon electronic tools and facilities

The parameters of the definition above were used as indicators to measure e-literacy awareness and readiness, which is when a person possesses ICT proficiency that is, working knowledge of how to use digital technology, communication tools and/or networks to define and recognize when information is needed, as well as how to access, manage, integrate and evaluate information. Correspondingly, e-literacy practices relate to the stage when a person demonstrates ICT proficiency as stated in terms of level of competency and frequency of ICT use and applications. In addition, they demonstrate the ability to create new information or knowledge and to be able to communicate this information to others (Azman, 2008). Finally it is recognized that :

Computer literacy + information literacy (+ moral or ethical literacy) = e-literacy.

4.3. E- LITERACY FOR LIS PROFESSIONALS

As educators of library users on E-literacy, librarians must first acquire e-literacy themselves. That is, LIS professionals should be conversant with courseware and networked information resources, and possess both knowledge and skills needed in a network environment. Besides the knowledge and skills in networked information described above as library users' network literacy, LIS professionals should further play multimodal role as:

- Adequate knowledge in globally recognizing, organizing and serving networked information resources and services;
- Adequate knowledgeable in creating, designing, organizing instructional programs for library users and for cooperative with teachers and computer/network specialists for network literacy curriculum;
- Adequate knowledgeable in online information in different subject fields to match the information needed with the problem solving;
- Familiar with different information systems and technology with different networked information available;
- Compatible with networking and computer technology related to information resources and services;
- Adequate knowledgeable in developing networked information resources and services;
- Skillful in operating computerized interfaces and other network facilities to access, use and process networked information (microcomputer operations, modems, multimedia devices, software applications, etc.).

Side by side LIS professionals have to acquire Knowledge in database management, system analysis and evaluation as well as project management for information services. The way for librarians to become self-literate for network literacy could be considered as:

- Self-learning through readings, professional conferences, networked information, and other self-learning channels.
- Professional learning from library and/or other professional schools as information professionals;
- Working on information services to gear up network literacy through hands-on practices; and

- Various training on media, computer, and network systems from continuing education, workshops, seminars, vendor training sessions, conferences and carrier advancement programme.

4.4. E-LITERACY FOR TECHNOLOGY ACCESS

E-literacy refers to various ICT tools along with their general functions and uses in the context of achieving the objectives. The context, content, methods and techniques as well as resources required for e-literacy may differ in particular at various organizations but in general, knowing the basic concepts of ICT using the computers for creating files, word processing, working with spreadsheets like excel and database, programming skills, software development and skills required for professional ICT specialization are important considerations for e-literacy in librarianship for putting knowledge to work.

E-literacy is a pre-requisite for applying technology effectively. It involves:

- *"Use technology as a tool to research, organize, evaluate and communicate information.*
- *Use digital technologies (computer, PDAs, Media Players, GPS, etc.) communication/networking tools and social network appropriately to access, manage, integrate, evaluate and create information to successfully function in a knowledge economy.*
- *Apply a fundamental understanding of the ethical/legal issues surrounding the access and use of information technologies"* Partnership for 21st Century skills is a national organisation of United States that advocates for 21st century readiness for every student <www.p21.org>.

4.5. ROLE OF LIS PROFESSIONALS IN E-LITERACY

4.5.1. Seminars or Workshop

Organization of seminars/conventions creates an opportunity for LIS professionals to provide e-literacy to user community in accordance of new technological development. Through seminars s/he provides information about library, various databases subscribed by library, various sources available in library, how to search databases, finally how to access information more easily, etc. Workshop also offers hands-on experience to recognize, evaluate and use of information as and when need.

4.5.2. Library Tours

Library tours are nothing but the process of taking user(s) inside the library by librarian. With this tour librarian gives information about whole library, arrangements of documents, databases, searching of OPAC, etc. Through a tour the user can be motivated to use the library resources.

4.5.3. Library Orientation Program

In this programs librarian gives orientation to new users, the orientation program covers following areas:

- Overview of library resources & services
- Way to use OPAC
- Way to use CD-Rom indexes
- Way to use multimedia encyclopedias, online searching of national and international databases.
- Expertise browsing of information resources, etc.

4.5.4. The Information Searching Course

Some LIS professionals arrange for a information searching skill course, such a course may cover following themes:

- Library collections, online and off-line mode
- Digital and virtual libraries
- Searching web based catalogues
- The intranet and internet
- The basic of web browser
- Search engines and specialized databases

- E-mail and e-mail discussion groups, archives
- Citing web and internet resources.

4.5.5. Online Library Tutorials

To gear up e-literacy some LIS professionals arrange online tutorials programmes. Online tutorials can be either interactive or read only format or PPT format.

4.6. SUPPORTS TOWARDS DEVELOPMENTS

4.6.1. Government Bodies

The University Grants Commission (UGC) has initiated a programme to provide electronic access over the Internet to scholarly literature in all areas of learning in the universities in India. The programme is wholly funded by the UGC. All universities which come under UGC's purview will be members of the programme, and it will gradually be extended to colleges as well. The programme is being executed by Director, Information and Library Network (INFLIBNET) Centre, Ahmedabad which is an autonomous institution under the UGC. Access to various E-Journals has started from January 1, 2004.

INFLIBNET initiate a project as part of ongoing international efforts to construct a networked digital library of theses and dissertations in all Indian University Libraries and it is presently accessible through its website.

The UGC has announced the Career Advancement Scheme (CAS) mandatory for the Assistant Librarian/College Librarians vide its letter no. F.3-1/94(PS)-7 dated 19.10.2006. Every Assistant Librarian in a University and a Librarian in a College, who is in the scale of pay of Rs.8000-275-13500, will be eligible for placement in a Senior Scale of Rs.10000-325-15200 through CAS. It is also applicable for the higher positions.

UGC Regulation on minimum qualifications for appointment of teachers and other academic staff in Universities and Colleges and Measures for the Maintenance of standards in Higher Education 2010 for consideration of promotion under career advancement scheme

(CAS) as per the provisions contained in the said UGC Regulation 2010 notified vide UGC letter No. F.3-1/2009 dated 30.6.2010 as per following :

From Assistant Librarian (Stage-1) to Assistant Librarian (Senior Scale) (Stage 2) in the PB-III (Rs. 15,600 to 39,100) with AGP Rs. 7000/-

From Assistant Librarian (Senior Scale) (Stage 2) to Assistant Librarian (Stage 3) in the PB-III (Rs. 15,600 to 39,100) with AGP Rs. 8,000/-

From Assistant Librarian (Selection Grade) to Deputy Librarian/Assistant Librarian (Selection Grade) (Stage 4) in the PB-IV (Rs. 37,400 to 67,000) with AGP Rs. 9,000/-

From Deputy Librarian (Stage 4) to Librarian (Stage 5) in the PB-I (Rs. 37,400 to 67,000) with AGP Rs. 10,000/-

The National Knowledge Commission, India has suggested the following points for LIS professionals realizing the changing roles in the society,

- Set up a National Commission on Libraries
- Prepare a National Census of all Libraries
- Revamp LIS Education, Training and Research facilities
- Re-assess staffing of libraries
- Set up a central library fund
- Modernize library management
- Encourage greater community participation in library management
- Promote Information Communication Technology (ICT) applications in all libraries
- Encourage Public Private Partnerships in LIS development.

While formally launching the "Knowledge Commission", the Prime Minister of India (October, 2005) said that it is the "Brain Power" which would be more powerful than military and economic power of a nation to determine a nation's place in the world now in making. The ability of a nation to make best use of its brain power will shape its place in the world in the present century. Building a knowledge economy and knowledge society was the only way to meet the challenges of Globalization and 21st century. Going beyond universities, colleges and schools, there are other elements of "Knowledge Economy". Public libraries are an extremely important element of the foundation of a knowledge economy.

4.6.2. Professional Organizations

Professional organizations should also play a great role to develop the professional efficiencies from time to time. It could host various seminars, workshops, hands-on trainings and refresher courses on new technologies. Professional organizations can keep up with changes in the profession and embrace it smoothly.

If we view the seminars / conferences that are organized by different LIS professional bodies of India we can definitely understand that the realization of multimodal roles of LIS professionals is well accepted. As for examples Indian Association of Special Libraries & Information Centres (IASLIC) has organized such topics since 2001. The table 7 below expresses the themes of different seminars / conferences of IASLIC:

Table 1. IASLIC Conference

Year	*Theme of the Conference*
2001	Content management in India in digital environment
2002	Digital information system & services
2003	Knowledge management in special libraries in digital environment
2004	Information support for rural development
2005	LIS profession in India: vision for 2010
2006	Open source movement: Asian perspective
2007	Digital media and library information services
2008	Library profession in search of a new paradigm
2009	Library/ Information users in digital era
2010	1. Reading habits in changing scenario 2. LIS education : emerging paradigm challenges and vision
2011	Library vision 2020
2012	Intellectual Property Rights: problems and prospects with special reference to library and information services

So from the above table it is clear that IASLIC has emphasized the present trends of LIS profession through its seminar / conference themes. Similarly it is visible in the themes of Society for Information Science (SIS), India, enlisted hereunder (Table 8):

Table 8 : SIS Conference

Year	*Theme of the Conference*
2003	Challenges in information management and e-learning in the age of globalisation: issues and opportunities
2004	Digital information exchange: pathways to build global information society
2005	Delivery of information services through distributed digital environment
2007	Webometrics, informetrics, scientometrics, science and society
2008	Role of librarian in 21st century
2009	Recent trends in patinformatics
2010	Open access gateway to open innovation
2012	Patinformatics for research and business planning
2012	Information, innovation & technologies : creating seamless linkages

Some of the leading associations or networks in India play a vital role for developing the Library and Information Science profession in different ways. A list of professional bodies with their respective websites is given below (Table 3):

Table 3. Library Associations and Networks in India

Sl No.	*Name of the Association Networks*	*Website*
1.	Ahmedabad Library Network (ADINET)	*http://www.alibnet.org*
2.	Bengal Library Association (Bangiya Granthagar Parishad)	*http://www.blacal.org/*
3.	Bombay Science Librarian's Association (BOSLA)	*http://www.bosla.org.in/*
4.	Delhi Library Association (DLA)	*http://www.dlaindia.org/*
5.	Developing Library Network (DELNET)	*http://delnet.nic.in/*
6.	Gujarat Library Association (Gujarat Granthalaya Seva Sangh – GGSS)	*http://ggss.org.in/*

7.	Indian Association of Special Libraries and Information Centers (IASLIC)	*http://www.iaslic1955.org/*
8.	Indian Library Association (ILA)	*http://www.ila-india.org/*
9.	Indian Theological Library Association	*http://www.geocities.com/itla_in/home.html*
10.	Information and Library Network (INFLIBNET)	*http://www.inflibnet.ac.in/*
11.	Kerala Library Association (KLA)	*http://www.keralalibraryassociation.org/*
12.	Madras Library Association (MLA)	*http://www.accel-india.com/mala/*
13.	Mysore Library Network (MYLIBNET	*http://www.mylibnet.org/*
14.	Society for Advancement of Library and Information Science (SALIS)	*http://autolib-india.net/salis.html*
15.	Society for Information Science (SIS)	*http://sis-india.netfirms.com/*

Functions of the LIS Associations include promoting interchange of information in the discipline of information science and its subdivision amongst the specialists and between specialists and the public; to encourage and assist the professionals to maintain the integrity and competence of the profession; to foster a sense of partnership amongst the professionals engaged in these fields; the furtherance of the library movement in India; the promotion of the training of librarians; and the improvement of the status of librarians.

4.6.3. LIS Schools

The preliminary tasks of LIS schools is to provide tactful teaching to give students of adequate knowledge and they also know how to develop a strategy for continuing their education once after completion their LIS school education specifically in real-field scenarios, how to develop skills for acceptance of new technologies and how to develop a strategy for troubleshooting technologies.

LIS schools definitely offered classes on evaluating software and using Internet how can traditional library services be provided from remote places in least possible time.

Studies pointed out the minimum responsibilities of LIS schools in this aspect are:

- Need based curriculum

- Competent faculty
- Instructional technology support
- Learning resources (print, electronic and web based)
- Continuing education programme
- System of continuous evaluation
- Adequate financial support from the sponsoring bodies.

The UGC Model Curricula (2001) recommended that "in view of the emerging network environment, in view of the fundamental shift in the goals of the library, and in view of the changes in information storage and delivery mechanisms, the educational programmes should cater the needs of these changed settings by including in their course contents, the knowledge and skills required to function effectively in such an environment".

This curriculum enumerated in detail the contents of each module along with objectives of the module and expected outcomes of the modules. Besides this, one important feature is that a part of the report contains a detailed syllabus for a 2-year integrated programme leading to MLIS along with the marking pattern, number of credits, number of hours of teaching theory and practice. Out of all the syllabi published so far, this syllabus seems to be useful and, therefore, soon after its publication, majority of the Indian universities have modified their course structure as per the recent report (2001). So now, almost all the university departments in India are having common syllabi for teaching the LIS subjects.

The following propositions are suggested for the LIS education in India:

- Provision of minimum infrastructure facilities by the controlling authority by giving sufficient funds.
- Assessment and accreditation of universities by any controlling organization at the national level to judge the quality of the products.
- Keeping a balance between the job opportunity and number of LIS products produced each year.

- Introduction of e-learning techniques to improve the quality of the products with minimum qualified teachers.
- Developing the competencies and confidence among the professionals by giving knowledge of latest technology.
- Keeping liaison between the LIS educationists and the library professionals for providing training in specialized courses.
- Making provision of modular courses for the new developments in the field.
- Giving more importance in deciding the research topics which should be related to the current issues such as "Need of LIS professionals in electronic environment, etc".

The e-literate person must be capable of making self-aware judgments during the processes of finding, evaluating, and explaining the information. A library and information centre with good e-literacy skills will manage information effectively, communicate appropriately internally and externally keep individuals up to date with new technologies, use information and technology for better organization.

In the changing paradigm, changing demands of users, changing nature of services, activities and functions in Librarianship enable us to be e-literate for making effective access to technology. Without e-literacy it is not possible to effectively exploit the benefits of ICT that helps to put knowledge to work. After all it recognized that the core objectives of LIS professionals are unchanged meanwhile to cope with the emerging technological development it is very much necessary to become knowledgeable in use of information technology.

REFERENCES

American Library Association. (1998). Final Report of Presidential committee on Information Literacy. Retrieved from at: *http://www.ala.org/ala/mgrps/divs/acrl/publications/whitepapers/presidential.cfm.*

Azman, Hazita. (2008). Social Transformation For the 21st Century: Impact of e-Community Centers on e-literacy in Rural Malaysia. Retrieved from *http://ieeexplore.ieee.org/xpls/abs_all.jsp?arnumber=4631986*

Halder, Sambhu Nath and Sarkhel, Juran Krishna. (2010). Bridging Between E-literacy and Library and Information Science Professionals. In H. S. Chopra

(Eds.), *Information Access Initiatives and Rural India* (pp. 498-510). New Delhi. Shree Publisher & Distributors.

INDIA. National Knowledge Commission. (2005). NKC recommendations on libraries: letter to the Prime Minister. Retrieved from *http://knowledgecommission.gov.in/downloads/ recommendations/LibrariesLetterP.pdf*

Koltay, T. (2007). A new direction for library and information science: the communication aspect of information literacy. *Information Research, 12*(4), 1-14. Professor T.D. Wilson. Retrieved from *http://search.ebscohost.com/login.aspx?direct=true&db=lxh&AN= 27511229&site=ehost-live*

Lloyd, Annemaree. (2003). Information Literacy: The Meta-Competency of the Knowledge Economy : An Exploratory Paper. *Journal of Librarianship and Information Science* 2003; 35; 87. Retrieved from *http://lis.sagepub.com/content/35/2/87.full.pdf+html* ,

Lupton, M., Glanville, C., McDonald, P. and Selzer, D. (2004). *Information Literacy Toolkit.* Brisbane, Queensland: Griffith University. Retrieved from *http://www.griffith.edu.au/ centre/gihe/griffith_graduate*

Martin, A. & Rader, H. (Eds). (2003). Information and IT literacy: Enabling learning in the 21st century. London: Facet Publishing.

Murthy, T. A. V., Cholin, V. S., Vijayakumar, J. K. (2005). UGC-INFLIBNET Initiatives in e-journal consortia and digital library of doctoral theses for Indian universities. *In proceedings of National Conference on Digital Library and e-Theses (NCDLET).* Kolkata Jadavpur University. Retrieved from *http://eprints.rclis.org/archive/ 00005658/01/vijayakumarjk_09.pdf*

University Grants Commission. (2001). UGC model curriculum: Library & Information Science. Retrieved from *http://www.ugc.ac.in/policy/modelcurr.html*

5

Issues Facing LIS Professionals

There is always a debate on the roles of libraries especially in the present era. The frequently asked questions are: i.) Are Libraries "inefficient, limited and obsolete" and ii). Is there a need for Libraries and Librarians in the electronic age?

We have already discussed that the various activities of LIS professionals in the light of present situation. But it should be kept in mind that professional and social acceptances of the profession depend upon the skills, attitudes and behaviors of the professionals. Due to the changes in the working environment of libraries the LIS professionals are facing challenges day by day. Not only in the internal activities of the libraries but the demands of the user's expectations are also changing relating to information and communication technologies. The users' expectations always seem to exceed library's capacity in terms of documents, infrastructure facilities, finance, staff etc. So, the LIS professionals have to choose whether he or she will manage and/or control the events that impact their workforce and produce stress or to allow stress to manage them.

Today's twenty-first-century library and information science (LIS) professionals are faced with the challenge of a growing population of individuals from diverse cultural backgrounds, many of whom are from minority and underserved population representing the poorest segments of society with little or no experience with libraries (Overall, 2009).

Most of the experts agree that in the future, libraries will place larger emphasis on customer services. LIS professionals will be specialists in locating, filtering, and evaluating information, and will be primary instructors in the use of new information technologies (Baruchson-Arbib & Bronstein, 2002).

5.1. APPROACHING KNOWLEDGE SOCIETY

The concept of the Knowledge Society and more specifically four criteria for a Knowledge Society - ICT infrastructure, information content, human intellectual capacity, and physical delivery infrastructure - are the main international issues.

5.1.1. ICT Infrastructure

A prerequisite for successful participation in the Knowledge Society is a well-developed, well-maintained and affordable information and communication infrastructure. Without such an ICT infrastructure global socio-economic activities and political participation are limited and even impossible. This ICT infrastructure can indeed be seen as the backbone of the information-based global economy.

5.1.2. Information Content

A well-developed and well-maintained information infrastructure is not sufficient unless it can provide access to relevant information needed to participate meaningfully in the dematerialized economy. Some of the prerequisites of relevant information include affordability, timeliness, and presentation in languages and contexts users can relate to and understand.

5.1.3. Human Capacity

It is our opinion that the investment in and development of human intellectual capability is one of the most important factor that facilitates further development and sound economic growth in the era of globalization. We argue that, if developing countries do not invest more in education they will be excluded from the global knowledge pool. "Human capital represents that property that allows people to live and work productively." It is of little use to have access to relevant information but not the educational infrastructural support, including R&D facilities, to enable people to create new knowledge.

5.1.4. Physical Delivery Infrastructure

The new information economy, to be efficient and effective, must be supported and underpinned by a material and efficient infrastructure. Amongst other things this includes well-maintained airports, railways, roads, warehouses and physical addresses of people. A dematerialized information-based economy without a physical infrastructure to allow the delivery of the physical products and rendering of services is of little use. In this connection it is increasingly being recognized that the digital divide is accompanied by an equally debilitating physical divide (Lor, Britz, 2007).

5.2. RECENT DEVELOPMENT IN LIS

Innovation of Information and Communication Technology has made a new era of library and information sector. The high speed data processing techniques, advancement in the storage medium and improved telecommunication systems have made profound impact in the library activities.

5.2.1. Collection Development

5.2.1.1 Open Access

Open access means the free availability of peer-reviewed literature on the public internet, permitting any user to read, download, copy, distribute or print without any restriction. The open access advantage has at least three components: (1) a citation count advantage (as a metric for knowledge uptake within the scientific community), (2) an end user uptake advantage, and (3) a cross-discipline fertilization advantage. As the advantages for publishing open access from a researchers' point of view become increasingly clear, questions around the sustainability of open access journals remain. Open source tools which have been developed by the Public Knowledge Project at the University of British Columbia with contributions from the Epublishing & Open Access group at the Centre for Global eHealth Innovation in Toronto are an alternative to hosting journals on commercial open access publisher sites (Gunther, 2006).

5.2.1.2. Institutional Repository

Looking at the concept of institutional repositories within the broader context of digital libraries, 'Institutional Repository' is an online locus for collecting, preserving, and disseminating in digital form, the intellectual output of and institution, particularly research institution. Digital libraries can mean many things, but we consider them to be libraries first and foremost, and built upon the enduring principles of information management which have lain at the heart of the practice of librarianship for hundreds of years. Libraries are themselves repositories, and have always dealt in the management of repositories for their users (MacColl, Jones, Andrew, 2006). Digital library software, DSpace, allows workflow and customization as per institutional requirements. It also supports community or collection based content and submission by different user communities.

5.2.1.3 E-journals

The term "Electronic Publishing" is not new to the academic community. The oldest use of the term documented by Willem Dijkhuis was probably the announcement of a conference organized in 1977 by US Institute of Graphic Communication. Joost Kist defined that "Electronic and optical publishing is the application by a publisher of computer added processes, by which international content is found, captured, shaped, stored and updated in order to judiciously disseminate it to a chosen audience". According to Reitz (2004) electronic journal is a digital version of a print journal, or a journal-like electronic publication with no print counterpart, made available via the web, e-mail, or other means of internet access. Some web-based electronic journals are graphically modeled on the print version. The rising cost of print journal subscriptions has led many academic libraries to explore electronic alternatives. Directories of electronic journals are available online (*example*: *Ejournal SiteGuide: a MetaSource* maintained by the University of British Columbia Library).

5.2.2. Library Consortia

A library consortium is described as a group of institutions or organizations who join together to fulfill a combined objective that requires co-operation and the sharing of resources. It is necessary to have a mutual understanding to ensure their success so that individual member can have more resources than individual capacity. Consortium is an association of independent libraries and/or library systems established by formal agreement, usually for the purpose of resource sharing. Membership may be restricted to a specific geographic region, type of library (public, academic, special), or subject specialization (Reitz, 2004). An alphabetical list of library consortia is maintained by 'LISWIKI' available at <liswiki.org/wiki/alphabetical_list_at_library_consortia).

5.2.3. Technological Development

5.2.3.1. RFID

RFID (Radio Frequency Identification) is an identification technology; it does the same job as bar codes but offers potentially a lot more. RFID is a term that is used to describe a system that transmits the identity of a book wirelessly, using radio waves. The use of microchips to tag library materials and the library card, enabling patrons to check out items by walking through a self-service station equipped with an antenna that emits low-frequency radio waves. When an RF tag (transponder) passes through the electromagnetic zone, a reader (antenna + transceiver) decodes the data encoded in the tag's integrated circuit, passing it to a computer that automatically links data from the physical item(s) to the patron record corresponding to the library card. Line-of-sight is not required for this noncontact system. RFID technology may eventually replace the barcode and optical technology in library circulation systems. Tags are available in various shapes and sizes for use in a wide range of applications, with read/write capability for interactive applications (Reitz, 2004). Strong technical and economic drivers compel the change from self-defined to infrastructure-managed RFID solutions. As the complexity of standalone reader deployment runs up against real-world scales of production, RFID is gravitating towards the standardized adaptations that have shaped earlier networking successes (Krishna, Husalc, 2007).

5.2.3.2. Barcode

A printed label containing machine-readable data encoded in vertical lines of equal length but variable thickness, which can be read into an attached computer by an optical scanner. The barcode is a Universal Product Code issued by the Uniform Code Council (UCC). In libraries barcodes are used to identify books and other materials for circulation and inventory and to link the borrower's library card to the appropriate patron record in automated circulation systems (Reitz, 2004). Barcode reader is optical scanner used for reading bar coded data (data in the form of light and dark lines). The bar coded data consists of a numbers of bars of varying thickness and spacing between them. The barcode reader reads the bar coded data and converts it into electrical pulses by computer. A research article of Cronin (2008) compares the effectiveness of radio frequency identification (RFID) and Barcode in capturing data. Studies reveal that RFID is as effective as Barcode in capturing the vital information need to be tracked. Some companies prefer to use RFID because it is capable to connect to a mobile computer equipped with a barcode scanner, while others find barcode as more accurate than RFID.

5.2.3.3. Web Technology

5.2.3.3.1. RSS

RSS is an acronym that stands for Rich Site Summary, though it's often alternatively defined as Really Simple Syndication. The simplest definition of RSS is an "eXtensible" Markup Language (XML) format that uses the Resource Description Framework (RDF) for representing information about resources on the World Wide Web. Similarly, Atom is another format based on XML technology.

In other words, according to Reitz (2004) RSS is a method of Web syndication, originally developed at Netscape, which uses XML file formats to publish frequently updated online works, such as blog entries, news headlines, and audio and video clips, in standardized format (see this example). An RSS document (called a *feed* or *web feed*) includes full or summarized text with limited metadata (usually publication date and author). The user subscribes to a feed by entering its URL into an *RSS reader* or by clicking a feed icon in a Web browser to initiate the subscription process. The RSS reader automatically checks the user's subscribed feeds on a regular basis, downloads any updates, aggregates them, and provides a user interface, enabling the subscriber to monitor and read new feeds at will without visiting multiple web sites. RSS readers are available for different platforms, or the user can select a web-based reader. RSS is a family of formats which allow users to find out the updates to the content of RSS enabled websites, blogs or podcasts without actually having to go and visit the site. Instead, information from the website and piped to the user in a process known as syndication. RSS stands for Rich Sites Summary, Really Simple Syndication, RDF (Resource Description Format) Site Summary or even Read Some Stories, depending on whom you talk to in order to be able to use a deed, a prospective user must install a software tool known as an aggregator or feed reader, onto their computer desktop.

5.2.3.3.2. Blog

The term web-log, or blog, was coined by Jorn Barger in 1997 and refers to a simple webpage consisting of brief paragraphs of opinion, information, personal diary entries or links, called posts, arranged chronologically with the most recent first, in the style of an online journal. Most blogs also allow visitors to add a comment below a blog entry. Weblog is a web page that provides frequent continuing publication of web links and/or comments on a specific topic or subject (broad or narrow in scope), often in the form of short entries arranged in reverse chronological order, the most recently added piece of information appearing first. An example in the field of library and information science is *LISNews.com*, which accepts postings from its readers. A list of library Weblog sites is maintained by Peter Scott on *Libdex* (Reitz, 2004). Blogs are using by the librarians to market the libraries and its services.

5.2.3.3.3. Library 2.0

Library 2.0 is a term coined by Michael Casey on his Library Crunch blog. It is "the application of interactive, collaborative, and multimedia web-based technologies to web-based library services and collections," and suggests this definition be adopted by the library science community (Gopikuttan, 2008). Jack Maness has an interesting piece over on Webology that explores the definition of Library 2.0. He presents a very well-argued thesis that Library 2.0 is primarily a technology-centered theory. While the technology does play a key role in the ability of today's library to move forward and serve more users, it is not convinced that technology can ever be the primary component in this thing we call Library 2.0.

Pushing such new technologies to users, either through in-house creation or from vendors, does little to create purposeful change in the library itself. Indeed, without continuous and purposeful change, how is the library to keep up with what its users want with regard to new technology? Technology is very important, but it is only a tool that will help us build Library 2.0 (Casey, 2006).

5.2.3.3.4. Web 2.0

While the term is widely defined and interpreted, Web 2.0 was reportedly first conceptualized and made popular by Tim O'Reilly and Dale Dougherty of O'Reilly Media in 2004 to describe the trends and business models that survived the technology sector market crash of the 1990s. Within 15 years the Web has grown from a group work tool into a global information space with more than a billion users. It is now entering a new more social and participatory phase. These trends have led to a feeling that the Web is entering a "second phase"- a new, 'improved' web version 2.0. This is also what Web 2.0 does – lets the people share information with each other easily. Geography is becoming less and less important, because some interaction happen online (Gopikuttan, 2008). Libraries are moving into web 2.0 in a surprisingly short-time.

5.2.3.3.5. Wikis

Wiki is a webpage or set of web pages that can be easily edited by anyone who is allowed access. A Wiki is a type of website that allows and encourages visitors to add, edit, change and hopefully improve on the existing content with the use of collaborative editing. Reitz (2004) stated that based on a Hawaiian term meaning "quick" or "informal." A web application that allows users to add content to a collaborative hypertext web resource (coauthoring), as Internet forum, and permits others to edit that content (open editing). Authorizations and passwords are not required, and content can be changed by anyone simply by clicking on a "edit" link located on the page. A wiki may have policies to govern editing and procedures for handling edit wars. Activity within the site can be watched and reviewed by any visitor to the site. The first wiki was the Portland Pattern Repository established by Ward Cunningham in March 1995. The term also refers to the collaborative server software used to collectively create such a web site, allowing web pages (stored in a database) to be easily created and updated. A prime example is *Wikipedia*.

5.2.3.3.6. Social Networking

It allows groups to work together by creating network of groups of people together to share knowledge, interests and experiences. Users are able to create their own profiles and share photographs, videos, journals and so on, create their own networks of friends and meet new people who share similar interests. Membership groups, associations, clubs, faith-based groups, families, political groups, school and alumni associations can all make use of social networking resources. Some popular social networking websites Academia.edu, Facebook, Flickr, hi5, ibibo, Netlog, Orkut, Twitter, etc.

Weaver and Morrison (2008) said that in the context of today's electronic media, social networking has come to mean individuals using the Internet and Web applications to communicate in previously impossible ways. This is largely the result of a culture-wide paradigm shift in the uses and possibilities of the Internet itself. The current web is a much different entity than the web of a decade ago. This new focus creates a riper breeding ground for social networking and collaboration. In an abstract sense, social networking is about everyone. The mass adoption of social-networking websites points to an evolution in human social interaction.

5.2.3.3.7. Mashup

Mashup is a web application that combines data from more than one source into a single integrated tool. Contents used in Mashup is typically sourced from a third party via a public interface or API (web serves); although some in the community believe that case where private interfaces are used should not count as Mashup. Mashup Cultures presents a broader view of the effects and consequences of current remix practices and the recombination of existing digital cultural content (Gopikuttam, 2008). 'WikiBios' for example, a site where users create online biographies of one another.

Mashups custom applications that combine multiple, disparate data sources into something new and unique are coming to the enterprise. Forrester projects that the enterprise mashup market will reach nearly 700 million by 2013; while this means that there is plenty of money to be made selling mashup platforms, it will affect nearly every software vendor. Mashup platforms are in the pole position and ready to grab the lion's share of the market and an entire ecosystem of mashup technology and data providers is emerging to complement those platforms. Those vendor strategists that move quickly, plan a mashup strategy, and build a partner ecosystem will come out on top (Young, Daley, Gualtieri, Lo, Ashour, 1995).

5.2.4. Tool & Techniques

5.2.4.1. OPAC/Web OPAC

Online Public Access Catalog is a library catalog consisting of a collection of bibliographic records in machine-readable format, maintained on a dedicated computer that provides uninterrupted interactive access via terminals or workstations in direct, continuous communication with the central computer. Although the software used in online catalogs is proprietary and not standardized, most online catalogs are searchable by author, title, subject heading, and keywords and most public and academic libraries in the United States provide free public access, usually through a Web-based graphical user interface (Reitz, 2004). Most important and popular OPAC is Library of Congress Online Catalogue available at <catalog.loc.gov/>.

5.2.4.2. FRBR

FRBR stands for Functional Requirements for Bibliographic Records. The principles are espoused in the 1998 report of the IFLA Study Group on Functional Requirements for Bibliographic Records. Although the report covers the user-oriented functions that bibliographic records should fulfill, and the data elements necessary to fulfill those functions, the term *FRBR* is usually used in reference to the entity-relationship model described in the report, which defines the characteristics of works, expressions, manifestations, and items.

In the years following the publication of *International Bibliographic Description for Monographic Publications* in 1971, major developments occurred in the environment in which cataloging principles and standards operate, such as the expansion of automated systems, the creation of large-scale bibliographic databases by national cataloging agencies, and the emergence of networked access to electronic information and new forms of electronic publishing, changes that necessitated a comprehensive re-examination of cataloging theory. In 1990, a resolution was passed at the Stockholm Seminar on Bibliographic Records calling for a clear delineation of the functions performed by the bibliographic record with respect to media, applications, and user needs (Reitz, 2004).

5.2.4.3. ISBN – 13

The ten-digit ISBN system had a theoretical numbering capacity of one billion. As ISBNs were assigned in over 150 countries, the rate of depletion accelerated, especially with the proliferation of new publishing formats. To increase numbering capacity, ISO introduced a thirteen-digit ISBN on January 1, 2007, identical to the EAN-13 barcode version of the ten-digit ISBN, which has an added three-digit prefix (978- for books) and a recalculated check digit. In the U.S., a five-digit add-on code is used in the publishing industry for price information, the lead digit identifying currency (5 for the U.S. dollar, 6 for the Canadian dollar, 1 for the British pound, and so on). In the United States, allocation of publisher prefixes and assignment of ISBNs is managed by Bowker. ISBN codes for publishers are listed in the *Publishers' International ISBN Directory available* from Bowker (Reitz, 2004). For example, ISBN-10 = 0-309-14436-1 corresponding to ISBN-13 = 978-0-309-14436-0.

5.2.4.4. Digital Object Identifier

Digital Object Identifier (DOI) is nothing but a unique code preferred by publishers in the identification and exchange of the content of a digital object, such as a journal article, Web document, or other item of intellectual property. The DOI consists of two parts: a prefix assigned to each publisher by the administrative DOI agency and a suffix assigned by the publisher that may be any code the publisher chooses. DOIs and their corresponding URLs are registered in a central DOI directory that functions as a routing system.

The DOI is persistent, meaning that the identification of a digital object does not change even if ownership of or rights in the entity are transferred. It is also actionable, meaning that clicking on it in a Web browser display will redirect the user to the content. The DOI is also interoperable, designed to function in past, present, and future digital technologies. The registration and resolver system for the DOI is run by the International DOI Foundation (IDF). CrossRef is a collaborative citation linking service that uses the DOI. Click here to learn more about the DOI (Reitz, 2004).

5.2.4.5. DDC – 22 / Web Dewey

Experience the power of the Dewey Decimal Classification (DDC) system on the Web! WebDewey gives access to an enhanced version of the DDC database.

The new WebDewey is easier to use than ever and features:

- All content from DDC 23, including regular updates (new developments, new built numbers, and additional electronic index terms)
- An easy-to-navigate, simple user interface that is suitable for the novice as well as the power user
- BISAC-to-DDC mappings
- An easy-to-personalize screen display, often done with a single click
- Continuous updating
- Links from mapped LCSH to the LCSH authority records.

Current WebDewey subscribers can access the new system with their existing authorizations and passwords. Web Dewey has more numbers than the print version as it is updated regularly.

Need to incorporate cuttering into workflows? Dewey Cutter Software automatically provides cutter numbers from the OCLC Four-Figure Cutter Tables (Cutter Four-Figure Table and Cutter-Sanborn Four-Figure Table) when input text. It works with Windows

Millennium, 2000, and XP, and is available for download at no charge (OCLC, 2012).

5.2.4.6. AACR 3

The Joint Steering Committee for Revision of AACR has embarked on an ambitious programme leading to a new edition of AACR, which is now being referred to informally, but publicly, as AACR3. The Joint Steering Committee for Development of RDA (JSC, 2007) is the new name of the Joint Steering committee for revision of AACR. The JSC was responsible for maintaining the Anglo-American Cataloguing Rules, and is now working a new code – "RDA: Resource Description and Access". The "AACR3" has the working title "Resource Description and Access" (Gopikuttan, 2008). Desoription of RDA is based on the conceptual model of FRBR, and Access Point Control is based on the FRAD (Functional Requirements for Authority Data).

5.3. FUTURE TRENDS

LIS professionals have done a commendable job in seizing new technology, but they will need to become much more aggressive and proactive in the future as they face increased competition from a variety of groups who think they can do a better job in providing information to the user. So in the near future the LIS professionals should have to take necessary responsibilities in:

(i) As providers of resources, they can help to enhance the amount of available resources by making stakeholders aware of the importance of sharing. In particular, as far as the sharing of content is concerned, they can operate by promoting digitization campaigns and the open access approach. These actions may result in a vast amount of new digital information accessible online which can be exploited by advanced services.

(ii) Within a digital framework, libraries are certainly the best candidates for carrying out content description, maintenance and preservation of resources. By exploiting their large experience acquired in the past, they can contribute to the long-term availability and to the quality of the resources disseminated by the digital libraries (DLs).

(iii) Long-term availability also requires the implementation of models able to support the sustainability of the resources provided. Libraries, either alone or as members of library consortia, can also act as the organizations deputed to define and put in place these models.

(iv) As main resource providers, libraries can work jointly on the definition of common policies and standards. An agreement on these aspects would strongly contribute towards facilitating the design and development of the new complex services required to fulfill the emerging user needs.

(v) In the future libraries can also play an important role as mediators between the infrastructure and the user communities. In particular, they can proactively promote and facilitate the creation of DLs that respond to the needs of the user communities. They can also assist users by providing, if necessary, the skills required to select, update and exploit the DL content and services (Castelli, 2006). It is not hard to realize that in near future library and information centres would be globalized and maximum services will be available from remote places.

The rapid pace of developments in the field of Information Technology and the advent of networked information services have prompted a comprehensive review of the Library and Information Science (LIS) profession. The technological developments of the past 25 years, such as electronic databases, on-line services, CD ROMs, and the introduction of the Internet, have radically transformed access to information, making information readily available, especially for the end user. However, the information overload is such that greater expertise is demanded in retrieving and analyzing relevant information. The information field has spread out of the libraries and information centers, and has been transformed into an industry that sells, organizes, and processes information.

Nowadays traditional roles of the library, such as, classifying and cataloging the books, preserving them and readers' services are changing rapidly. Library schools in the globe have confronted technological challenges and adapted their curriculum according to the new developments. In addition, many academic research studies discuss expected changes that the LIS profession is undergoing. Among the central questions raised is the issue of disintermediation. In other words, will the easy access to information completely eliminate the need for the librarian as an intermediary? Another important question concerns the possible transformation of the traditional library into a virtual entity with the majority of the information in electronic format. The Web is not a library substitute, and that there will always be a need for libraries and librarians to help users cope with the ever-changing information environment. However, the LIS profession will certainly change, and the LIS schools will have to meet these developments and change their study programs. The major cause for change in the libraries is, of course, the Internet. The World Wide Web consists of an enormous amount of disorganized information, which may appear easy to use at first glance but can also be confusing. First, the vast amount of retrievable information one can obtain from an Internet search gives the impression that one has plumbed the depths of available information on a given topic. This is not true, because the proportion of available digital content is minute compared to the amount of printed materials available. Furthermore, many printed resources are so large that complete digital conversion is not possible. Second, much of what is available on the Web does not conform to reasonably accepted standards of validation. A significant amount of web material has been "published" by individuals, without peer review or institutional affiliation. Third, there exists a minimal collection structure or organization. The information retrieved by a researcher from the internet depends on the adequacy of the search engines and data bases used, and on the user's skills in using those (Griffiths, 1999). Today there is a need for skilled librarians who are specialists in managing, retrieving, filtering, and evaluating information. Just as a person walking into a library for the first time must learn to translate the organizational design into the ability to find a book on a shelf, anyone using database must be trained to appreciate the value and benefits of a similar investigative process (Adams, 1997). Today, many users start out searching on their own and then come back to the LIS professional for help and advice when they are tangled in an irrelevant flood of information (Schulman, 1998).

There are two vital issues within the LIS profession; one is collection of information that may be in written, printed, and electronic formats and other is the intellectual "tool set" - the skills embodied in the staff and their activation into tasks such as cataloging, indexing, and reference work. Looking at a library as a concept rather than a place begins to open up our thinking about the future roles of LIS professionals. It is important that we start to draw our attention away from the collections, the objects, and look at the special services that LIS professional provide (Panel, 1990).

An eminent personality, Virginia Walsh (2010) has given a pictorial presentation on the future of the library profession and highlighted various innovative issues that reflect the LIS profession. These are discussing hereinafter under different headings.

5.4. CYBERSPACE

The advancement of Information and Communication Technology (ICT) has bred a new lexicon. Librarians have been called warriors on the information superhighway, cybrarians and navigators in the knowledge economy. While few can legitimately claim such status in cyberspace, all need to aspire to this goal. These new information technologies provide threats and opportunities to the global library community.

All LIS professionals are not keen to have embraced new technologies volitionally. A small and inadequate amount of resources matched with inadequate or inappropriate training has made the choice difficult for many people. Some have been swept along on the tide of technological change unsure of where the journey ends. Copyright, preservation, legal deposit, privacy, content regulation and censorship are all issues which need to be resolved quickly and thoughtfully.

5.5. CONTENT REGULATION

LIS professionals are familiar with the comment about the lack of road signs on the 'information superhighway'. Librarians, as access providers, are grappling with the problems of Internet regulation as the push for access to digital information outpaces the development of public policy solutions.

The regulatory challenge in digital content regulation in a digital setting was to find appropriate legislative and other mechanisms to safeguard policy objectives. The shift in the regulatory mechanism implied self-regulation, on the one hand, self-regulation had different meanings depending on the sector, while on the other hand, the 'self' of self-regulation was difficult to determine, as the Internet industry was not monolithic, with a single 'industry' that spoke for the whole media form. If the function of self-regulation was to minimize harmful and illegal conduct on the Internet, particularly as it affected young people, it was suggested to become more extensive. The development of a self-regulatory regime for digital services could have been composed of multiple complementary actions, tools, and mechanisms. A new phenomenon of re-intermediation was emerging as the abundance of content had led to the creation of new types of mediation and hence new intermediaries (e.g. electronic programme guides, portals, and search engines). Information exiles may have resulted if no regulatory paradigm was reconsidered (Verhulst, 2006). Many libraries are facing the challenges to develop and manage an institutional repository. Genoni (2004) addresses the issue of content in repositories, and suggests that librarians need to approach the task of content development by applying some of the procedures and skills associated with collection management within more traditional environments. The types of content that might be suitable for institutional repositories, and several recent Australian reports have recommended the need for a more standardized and regulated approach to the content of institutional repositories. It is argued that this is inappropriate.

5.6. COPYRIGHT

Copyright is the exclusive legal rights granted by a government to an author, editor, compiler, composer, playwright, publisher, or distributor to publish, produce, sell, or distribute copies of a literary, musical, dramatic, artistic, or other work, within certain limitations (fair use and first sale). Copyright law also governs the right to prepare derivative works, reproduce a work or portions of it, and display or perform a work in public (Reitz, 2004).

Gallart (2000) analysed two main developments like, the expansion of licensing and libraries as hosting/publishing services. While stressing the importance of copyright issues, the final conclusion is that management and ownership of digital collections, distributed all over the world, is the only way for libraries to survive and to have a chance to fulfill their mission in the digital environment. In the international context the mechanisms for dealing with copyright are well established. The Berne and Universal Copyright Conventions provide the model for the development of national rules that govern the granting of these rights. But the development of new technologies is challenging the traditional controls applying to the 'old media'.

Now a days dealing with copyright is a complex task. The abundance of legal jargon, multiplicity of international bodies, economic repercussions and political interests all contrive to distract people. Distribution, communication and reproduction rights in the digital universe require a concerted intellectual commitment on the part of librarians around the world. Copyright problems cannot be solved in a patchwork manner now that information flows are more than ever globalize. International associations have a great role in developing acceptable solutions.

5.7. TRADITIONAL ROLES

As the demand for on-line services in the Third World advances, problems remain with meeting traditional library services at the most basic levels of developing and maintaining collections. The pressure to accommodate traditional library services, education and training courses and to link up to on-line services is beyond the means of these nations. While the information community has demonstrated an obsession with on-line communications technologies in recent years, one only has to step into a suburban library to know that in reality, the provision of traditional library services predominate. Dependence on traditional paper-based materials is also predominant in university, school and special libraries. Acquisitions, cataloguing and reference services are still provided. Paper-based materials are repaired and maintained. Managers in libraries have to hire and fire staff, develop budgets, draw up strategic plans, search for sponsorship and market their libraries. In the international community we are all enriched by the opportunity to work together for the common good. Improving the quality of library services is a priority for all LIS professionals and a responsibility that would be accepted by those beyond the library profession.

5.8. SENSE OF COMMUNITY

The advent of the virtual library is usually presented as a welcome development for library users. Unfortunately, the emphasis which is often placed upon convenience of access tends to reinforce the perception of the use of information resources as a solitary activity. In fact, information retrieval (IR) in the conventional library is often a highly collaborative activity, involving users' peers and experts such as librarians. Failure in the design of virtual library services to take into account the ways in which physical spaces help engender a sense of community and facilitate collaboration will result in its users being denied timely and effective access to valuable sources of assistance (Procter, McKinlay, Goldenberg, Davenport, Burnhill, Cannell, 1997). One of the great characteristics of the domestic and international library scene is the impressive sense of community that exists within the profession of librarianship. This sense of community is a source of great strength but, importantly, it must not distract us from the need to develop effective partnerships with other members of the information sector - such as the archivists - and with other organisations beyond our sector which can assist us move our agenda forward into the future.

Libraries do play a fundamental role in the development and maintenance of a good society. They are not an anachronism in the brave new world of cyberspace but balance the demands of maintaining our cultural heritage, assist in the development of literacy, provide an adjunct to education and training, serve as community and recreation centres and are an attraction to tourists. With expanded access to information using digital technology the demand for library services is growing. Librarians cannot ignore the necessity of responding to community and business enthusiasm for more colourful, animated, interactive and timely information. Targeting the right information, developing information literacy and navigating the 'superhighway' will be done through libraries just as we continue to meet the more traditional demands for library services. There is a risk that present and future demands will create a greater chasm between the information rich and information poor of the local and global community. But there is, as never before, the capacity to bridge this gap (Walsh, 2010). Bookmobiles and homebound delivery services flourish the library's reach and offer seniors and persons with disabilities the same experiences they would get by visiting personally. Libraries can also build relationships between community members and reach to provide services for all people without consideration of ages and backgrounds.

5.9. DIGITAL PRESERVATION

Long term preservation of documents is now hot issue in the present time. Accessioning to the digital documents in twenty or hundred years from now will be out of the question, if people not process the bit steam underlying digital documents. Digital documents are not fragile. There is a different between paper and digital records, any paper record can be perceived through the five human senses, but no digital records can be perceived without going through the computers hardware and software (Hagg, 2002). The speed of technological obsolescence makes digital preservation an important issue for everyone.

Digital preservation is concerned with ensuring that records which are created electronically using today's computer systems and application remain available, usable and authentic in future use, so digital preservation consist of preserving more than just the records bit stream for interpret the survival of the records otherwise without interpretation the bit stream is nothing more than a meaningless series of 0's and 1's (Hagg, 2002). During preservation question of record context, content, structure, appearance and behaviors must be taken into account which can be solved by standardizing the context, content, structure, format, appearance, etc. Standardization is in itself promising to slow down the speed of the ageing process because, standardization is the setting up by authority of common consent of a quality, quantity, pattern, method on unit of measurement for adoption as a common minimum or as a n example of imitation (AS 4390, 2001). Thus standardization is indispensable for different aspects of preservation. In fact, there is no standard explicitly designed for digital preservation.

5.9.1. Method of Digital Preservation

5.9.1.1. Digital preservation

The preservation of digital resources is finding ways to maintain our digital heritage, whether it exists in the form of e-journals, database records, websites-mails, digital images, audio-visual materials, interactive programmes or any other kind of binary data. Digital preservation is defined as consisting of a set of managed activities that will (a) ensure the long term maintains of a byte stream sufficient to reproduce the document and (b) Provide continued accessibility of the contents over time and through evolving technology. According to Cornell University Library, "Digital Preservation encompasses a broad range of activities designed to extent the usable life of machine readable computer files and protects them from media failure, physical loss and obsolescence". According to Russell (1998) digital preservation is a process by which digital data is perceived in digital form in offer to ensure the usability, durability and intellectual integrity of the information contained therein. The most precise concept is the storage, maintenance and accessibility of a digital material over a long term, usually as a consequence of applying one or more digital preservation strategies. These strategies may include technology preservation, technology emulation or date migration.

5.9.1.2. Preservation of Digital Materials

Digital media, no doubt, have immense capacity to record information enabling the libraries to provide users seem-less access to information, but it is very fragile in comparison to print media. Archiving of digital information is more complicated than archiving printed information.

Digital preservation means taking steps to ensure the longevity of the electronic document in terms of the following (Mark; 1999)

- Data (this might be for text, image, video or audio stored in variety of format and standards)
- Index to the data
- Link to other data
- Metadata
- Software (relies upon hardware and operating System)
- Storage medium

Hence, in the preservation of digital heritage material the following measures taken into account :

- Integrity of digital materials
- Physical presence
- Preservation format
- Digital materials functionality
- Location and reference of digital materials
- Authenticity of the materials and
- Provenance.

5.9.1.3. Standards for Digital Preservation

Standardization is the process of formulating and applying rules for an orderly approach to a specific activity for the benefit and with the co-operation of all concerned and in particular for the promotion of optimum overall economy taking a due account of functional condition and safely. Thus standardization is the secrete behind quality uniformity of measurement, norms, terminology which directly affect mass production that leads to economy of time, space , efforts, material, manpower and money and facilitates and acts as a tool of transfer of information which is required for digital information preservation (Dempsey; 1998).

5.9.1.4. Standards for Architecture

In a distributed digital environment the management of digital collection cannot be responsibility of just one central organization. In such environment it is important to agree on concepts, definitions and procedures. For this there are several standards on record management architecture.

5.9.1.4.1. ISO/DIS 15489

ISO/DIS 15489 is a draft international standard on record management and this standard enable organizations to standardize the following measures:

- The terms and definition used in record management system
- Regulatory environment
- Policies and responsibilities
- Design and implementation of record system
- Record management process and controls
- Record monitoring and auditing
- Record management training

5.9.1.4.2. AS 4390

In December 1995, Australia became the first country in the world to develop a standard on records management, i.e. AS 4390 - 1996. Following the approval and release of the standard, the international records management community began work on the development of an International Standard. This work used AS 4390 -1996 Records Management as its starting point. AS ISO 15489-2002 replaces AS 4390-1996 (State Records of South Australia, 2009).

5.9.1.4.3. DOD 5015.2.STD

The *DOD* 5015.2 *STD* is being developed by Department of Defense of USA. It is a similar type of standards as *ISO/DIS* 15489 or *AS* 4390 for the record management system. The*DOD* 5015.2 STD implementing and procedural guidance on the management of document management system (DoD, 2001).

5.9.1.4.4. OAIS (Open Archival Information System)

The Open Archival Information System is developed by the Consultative Committee for space data system (CC SDS) of the NASA. The OAIS reference model described both the information flow and archival requisite and it is being reviewed as an *ISO/DIS*. This architecture is implemented by various types of digital library and archives (OSAIS, 2001).

5.9.1.5. Standards for preservation Content

Standards for preservation content should be depending upon ageing process of the semantic and physical recoverability of the document that is being preserved. A standard can only provide such longevity when the standard itself does not change and backward compatibility is provides. Therefore for future preservation standard should be selected depending upon the technical obsolesces. More often *XML* and *PDF* are put forward as two rivals to preserve a document for long term preservation (Haag, 2002).

5.9.1.5.1. PDF (Portable Document Format)

Portable Document Format is the de facto document standard and is the proprietary of Adobe. It uses the image model of the post script language in order to depict text and image as exact copies of the original. The PDF have two types of format (Arora; 2004).

- Text based PDF outline font technology of postscript PDL (Page Description Language) for describe format of a page and
- Roster scanned image PDI without text outline font OCR (Optical Character Recognition)

5.9.1.5.2. XML (Extensible Mark-up Language)

Extensible mark-up language is a de facto standard rather than an official one. XML is subset of the standard SGML (Standard Generalized Mark-up Language) and is related to the web language HTML Hypertext Mark-up Language and is related to the web language HTML Hypertext Mark-up language (XML, 2001). With the help of the XML the structure of a document can be saved in a specific type document so called document, type description (DTD). For the specification of the form of document style sheet can be used. Cascading style sheet (CSS), extensible style sheet language (XSL) or XSL transformation (XSLT) can be used. Finally the content of the document can be stored is ASCII format with XML "tags" (Hagg; 2002).

5.9.1.6. Standards for Preservation Access

Preservation of the bit stream of the document in some standard format is not enough to preserve a digital document over a indefinite period of the time, so it is necessary for the description of the digital, object or various parts into one object means file/ formats stored in different physical places in the information system and linked by cross reference. Such types of descriptions are called metadata which included the contextual information to manage, retrieve and interpret the electronic information over time (Dempsey, 1998). Metadata gives information about both preserved document and information about the data processes of the digital objectives that are to be preserved by informing about format name, structure, application etc. (Lupvici and Masanes, 2000).

5.9.1.6.1. Dublin Core

The Dublin Core has especially been developed for cross

disciplinary network discovery. Its current status is Draft American National Standard and has been given the much revealing name ANSI/ NISO Z39.50 (DC; 1999). It exists upon 15 elements (i.e. Title, Creator, Subject, Description, Publisher, Contributor, Date, Type, Format, Identifier, Source, language, Relation, Coverage, and Rights) for resources description and discovery.

5.9.1.6.2. MARC

The machine readable standards are under supervision of the machine readable bibliographic information committee in conjunction with network development and MARC standard office library of Congress. MARC defines the representation and communication of bibliographic and relation definition in machine readable forms. Machine records contain a guide to its data or little "sign post" before each piece of bibliographic (Furriee, 1998). MARC is starting point for metadata description. MARC is industry wise standard, therefore it facilitates permanent access to records.

5.9.1.6.3. ISAD (G)

For defining and managing access to actual content a standard ISAD (G) general International Standard Archival Description is most suitable. It contains general rules for archival description. *ISAD(G)* is based on 27 elements and multilevel starting with general level to the less specific series level which is subdivided into files consisting of atoms and it represents the structure of the archive in relation to the context of description (ISAD; 1999). Six mandatory data elements are, (i) Reference Code, (ii) Title, (iii) Name of Creater, (iv) Date of Creation, (v) Extent of the chief of description, (vi) Level of descriptions.

5.9.1.6.4. Z39.50

Z39.50 is an ANSI/NISO standard for information storage and retrieval under supervision of the Z39.50. Maintenance Agency (Library of Congress) of Z39.50 and its possible successor ISO 23950 is a protocol which specifies data structure and enable searching or interchanging bibliographic information on different platform in a distributed environment (Arora; 2004). The Z39.50 Target Directory contains all the ANSI/NISO 239.50 (ISO 239.50) and SRU/SRW target known to us. Available at IRSY website <irspy.indexdata.com>.

5.9.1.7. Standards for Interoperability

Interoperability is ability of multiple systems with different hardware or software platform, data structure and interface to exchange data with minimum loss of content and functionality. Therefore interoperability is a critical problem in the network environment with increase in diverse computer systems software applications, file formats, information and users. But it is important for digital preservation in digital library and archives.

5.9.1.7.1. ODMA (Open Document Management API)

The Open Document Management API enables integration of proprietary document application into ODMA compliant document management system. Now many document management software packages are already ODMA complaint (ODMA; 1994). To determine the vital information can pass between applications, it is important that there be some sort of common interface – a translation device that can allow applications to understand each other's data formats and successfully access their documents. The Open Document Management API is such an interface. Basically ODMA was among the first attempts to integrate applications, and it paved the way for a number of other open standards that have further revolutionized document management, such as WebDAV.

5.9.1.7.2. DMA (Document Management Alliance)

The DMA is a comprehensive standard for interoperability among electronic document management systems (EDMSs). The Document Management Alliance tries to solve the problem of island of information that created different proprietary DMSs (Document Management Software), e.g. MS-Word. DMA creates bridges between these island on protocol level by facilitating client to access several different DMA compliant DMS through one DMA server in a network environment (DMA; 1997).

5.9.1.7.3. WebDAV (World Wide Web Distributed Authoring and Versioning)

The web distributed authoring and versioning is an interoperability standard, where HTTP is used to read network documents. The WebDAV enables author to write (Upload) document element by extending HTTP protocol. It also enables distributed network environment (WebDAV; 2001). The WebDAV extensions support the use of HTTP for interoperable publishing of a variety of content, providing a common interface to many types of repositories and making the web analogous to a large-grain, network-accessible file system.

Digital preservation in all its aspects is going to require some form of organizational transformation. Standards are essential for digital preservation. Though they were not developed for digital longevity, standards facilitate communication and acceptance and are useful to delay ageing process. The information and communication technology industry should be made aware of the need to take preservation requirements into account. The value of standards and open source software should be promoted among software developers. Standards are many in number depending upon different purpose. In real field scenarios the issues related to the digital preservation are those increasing complication of digital objects and their increasing software dependence, the increasing number of digital objects and proliferation of document standards and formats. Consideration of long-term access requirements when creating digital products and widely-accepted standards that will assure access overtime are so vital. Nevertheless, long term solutions to the problems require cooperation across traditional boundaries to include the experience gained inside and outside of the library and information centre (Halder, Das, 2012).

5.10. MARKETING OF INFORMATION PRODUCT AND SERVICES

Now the day's information is treated as commodity. There is a need to recognize the value, importence and utility of marketing of information product and services in the network era and information society of the 21st century. Library and Information Centres in the new changing paradigm must transform by adopting the information and communication technology as a tool in information organisation and services. LIS professionals need to build information resources in the new medias, use of technologies for information retrieval in the changing information needs of the users and enhancing the optimum use of the library and information centres and resources.

5.11. OPEN SOURCE SOFTWARE

In 1998 the Open Source Initiative was formed and it has developed the definition of Open Source Software, based on ten criteria that must be fulfilled in order for software to be considered as open source:

- Free Redistribution – can sell or give away software.
- Source Code – must be included and allowed to be redistributed.
- Derived Works – allows modifications to be released with same terms.
- Integrity of the Author's Source Code – restrictions on redistribution of modified source code only if license allows distribution of patch files with source code.
- No discrimination against persons or groups
- No discrimination against fields of endeavor – example: no restrictions against use in genetic research or business.
- Distribution of License
- License must not be specific to a product – cannot insist on particular software package.
- License must not restrict other software – example, no insistence

that all other programs are OSS.

- License must be technology-neutral – cannot insist on particular technology or style or interface.

Open Source Software is not a strange thing and at the same time is also not a familiar thing to libraries. There is still some scepticism among the library community regarding this kind of software. But with the increasing awareness about the OSS, the library community is becoming more and more interested to use it in the libraries. OSS has been developed to facilitate many library related tasks such as cataloguing photographs and managing bibliographies. There are many advocates in the library community for using OSS in libraries. Libraries are seeking alternatives to proprietary applications which may require specialized support and/or services. Moreover, OSS and proprietary products have a functional verisimilitude, and, as proprietary applications developers anticipate user needs, so too do OSS contributors. Practical implications of the degree of variance between proprietary and OSS applications, features, support, and compatibility is continually lessening, so libraries are increasingly making use of less costly alternatives to subscription based tools (Morgan, 2002). Using open source software is as good as owns it. It is a suitable candidate for long term library use and it is also worth of spending time and energy on learning and adopting. LIS professionals still believe in closed source commercialized solutions. But with the growing popularity and use of open source software in the libraries world wide, the Indian libraries will not be lagged far behind in using this open source code and open source software.

5.12. REQUIRED SKILLS FOR LIS PROFESSIONALS

The electronic environment of the 21st century will demand a range of skills from by Library and Information Science (LIS) professionals, including:

(i) Technical skills.

(ii) Information Technology (IT) skills.

(iii) Managerial skill (Sridhar, 2004).

This is to be considered that interpersonal skills, behavioural characteristics and technical services skills are in demand world wide. Various competencies are enabling LIS professionals to make library services effective in this ever changing Information Age. In this regard, Farkas (2006) said that if librarians can adapt to and embrace change, can easily learn technologies, can keep up with changes in the profession, can plan for new services and evaluate old services, can develop services that meet the needs of all stakeholders, can evaluate technologies, and can sell their ideas and market services they will be better able to meet the challenges of changing user populations and changing technologies.

According to National Knowledge Commission, India, skills required for fulfilling the changing role of libraries are:

(i) Library and information handling skills.

(ii) Service orientation.

(iii) ICT knowledge skills.

(iv) Communication and training skills.

(v) Marketing and presentation skills.

(vi) Understanding of cultural diversity.

(vii) Knowledge mapping skills

All pervasive information technology (e-world) has affected significantly the rendering of library and information services, but adoption of IT to library services has not been smooth. In addition to professional knowledge, librarianship is expected to have some knowledge in the areas of management, foreign languages, statistics, computers, etc. New professionals of e-world of 21st century need to have not only knowledge and skill in the areas of information technology but also matching "will" to carryout the services in the new media and means. Any significant gap between knowledge and corresponding skills required is dangerous (Sridhar, 1999).

Meredith Farkas (2006) mentioned in her blog entitled "skills for the 21st century librarian" some of important competencies, which librarians should adopt to cope up with the changing paradigm of

LIS profession.

A. *Basic Tech Competencies*
   i. Ability to embrace change
   ii. Comfort in the online medium
   iii. Ability to troubleshoot new technologies
   iv. Ability to easily learn new technologies
   v. Ability to keep up with new ideas in technology and librarianship (enthusiasm for learning)

B. *Higher Level Competencies*
   i. Project management skills
   ii. Ability to question and evaluate library services
   iii. Ability to evaluate the needs of all stakeholders
   iv. Vision to translate traditional library services into the online medium
   v. Critical of technologies and ability to compare technologies: ability to sell ideas/library services

Change is inevitable. If LIS professionals can adapt to and embrace change, they can easily learn innovative technologies, can keep up with changes in the profession and can develop services that meet the needs of all stakeholders.

Function of the librarians is developing to that of information access provider, intermediary, organizer and preserver of digital information, and web developer, etc. To perform such roles, the librarians have to adopt their traditional skills of collecting, organizing and retrieving information as well as possess some enhanced skills and competencies to perform their role effectively to the digital environment. LIS courses should be geared to the changing needs of the society and offer such courses to provide graduates with necessary skills and competencies. As said Myborgh (2004) that with skills and competencies LIS professionals can gain employment upon graduation as well as the vision and understanding which might help them to cope better with the rapidly changing would in which we live.

REFERENCES

Arora, J. (2004). Building Digital Libraries: an overview. *Conference Proceeding of INFOGOLD*. BIT, Mesra.

Baruchson-Arbib, S., & Bronstein, J. (2002). A view to the future of the library and information science profession: A Delphi study. *Journal of the American Society for Information Science and Technology, 53*(5), 397-408. Retrieved from *http://doi.wiley.com/10.1002/asi.10051*

Casey, Michael. (2006). Service for the Next Generation Library: A Library 2.0. *LibraryCrunch*. Retrieved from *http://www.librarycrunch.com/2006/08/_library_20_theory_web_20_and.html*

Choudhury, B. K. and Pradhan, D. K. (2005). Standards for digital preservation for Longevity: an approach. *Paper presented at SIS conference*. A. P. University, Visakhapattnam.

Cronin, Ray. (2008). RFID versus Barcode. *Pharmaceutical Technology, 32*(11), 177-178. Retrieved from *http://search.ebscohost.com/login.aspx?direct=true&db=bth&AN=35372953&site=ehost-live*

Dempsey, L. & Heery, R. (1998). Metadata: a current view of practice and issues. *Journal of Documentation*. (54) 2, 145 – 172.

Directory of Open Access Repositories. (2006). Retrieved from *http://www.opendoar.org/ index.html.*

Eysenbach, Gunther. (2006). The Open Access advantage. *Journal of medical Internet research, 8*(2), Retrieved from *http://eprints.ecs.soton.ac.uk/21856/1/Swan_%2D_Cologne_Dec_2010.pptx*

Farkas, M. (2006). Skills for the 21st century librarian. *Information wants to be free blog*. Retrieved from *http://meredith.wolfwater.com/wordpress/2006/07/17/skills-for-the-21st-century-librarian/*

Gallart, N. (2000). The Future of Copyright Management: Library Perspectives. *Proceedings of IFLA General Conference and Council*, (66). Retrieved from *http://www.ifla.org/IV/ifla66/papers/172-184e.htm*

Genoni, P. (2004). Content in institutional repositories : a collection management issue. *Library Management, 25*(6), 300-306. Retrieved from *http://www.emeraldinsight.com/10.1108/01435120410547968*

Gopikuttan, A. (2008). Current developments in library and information services. *Journal of Information Science and Technology*, 1*(1)*.

Haag, D. (2002). XML and Digital Preservations. Retrieved from *http://www.digitaleduc.zamhind.xl/does/xml.pdf*

Halder, Sambhu Nath and Das, Prodip. (2012). Open source software evolution and its impact on the library. In N C Ghosh and Parthasarathi Mukhopadhyay (Eds.), *Open Access: Gateway to open innovation* Kolkata : Society for information science (pp. 397-405).

Halder, Sambhu Nath. (2011). Digital Preservation Standards in Librarians' Point of View. In Mange Ram and Ram Chander (Eds.), *Recent Trends in Library Services*. New Delhi: Vayu Education of India. (pp. 167- 178)

Howard, K. (2010). Programming Not Required: Skills & Knowledge For The Digital Library Environment. *Australian Academic Research Libraries, 41*(4), 260-275

ISO/DIS 15489 on Records Management. (2001). International Organization for Standardization, Geneva. Retrieved from *http://www.iso.ch.*

Joint Steering Committee for Revision of AngloAmerican Cataloguing rules. (2007). RDA : Resource Desoription and Access. Retrieved from www.collectionscanada.ca/jse/rda.html

Kaur, Amritpal. (2007). Preservation of Digital Heritage Materials in the 21st Century. *SRELS Journal of Information Management,* 44 (4).

Krishna, P , Husalc, D. (2007). RFID Infrastructure. *IEEE Communications Magazine.* Retrieved from *http://ieeexplore.ieee.org/lpdocs/epic03/wrapper.htm?arnumber=4342872*

Lupovici, C. & Masanes, J. (2000). Metadata for long term preservation of electronic publications. Den Haag: Koninklijke Bibliotheek.

MacColl, John, Jones, Richard D, Andrew, Theo. (2006). The institutional repository in the digital library. *Writing.* Chandos (Oxford) Publishing Ltd. (pp. 1-30) Retrieved from *http://hdl.handle.net/1842/858*

Morgan, E. L. (2002). Open source software in libraries. *Library Review, 59*(9), 105-107. Retrieved from *http://www.emeraldinsight.com/journals.htm?issn=00242535&volume=59&issue=9&articleid=1891981&show=abstract*

National Digital Preservation Programme. (2011). Centre of Excellence for Digital Preservation. Retrieved from *http://www.ndpp.in/*

OCLC. (2012). The easiest way to use DDC. Retrieved from *http://www.oclc.org/dewey/versions/webdewey/default.htm*

Overall, P. M. (2009). Cultural competence: A conceptual framework for library and information science professionals. *Library Quarterly, 79*(2), 175-204. Retrieved from *http://universityofarizona.worldcat.org.ezproxy2.library.arizona.edu/title/cultural-competence-a-conceptual-framework-for-library-and-information-science-professionals/oclc/423662910&referer=brief_results*

Procter, R., McKinlay, A., Goldenberg, A., Davenport, E., Burnhill, P., & Cannell, S. (1997). Enhancing community and collaboration in the virtual library. *Information Sciences.* Springer -Verlag. Retrieved from *http://researchrepository.napier.ac.uk/3151/*

Reitz, Joan M. (2004). Online Dictionary for Library and Information Science.

Retrieved from *http://www.abc-clio.com/ODLIS/searchODLIS.aspx*

Russell, Kelly. (1998). CEDARS: Long-term Access and Usability of Digital Resources. Retrieved from *http://www.ariadne.ac.uk/issue18/cedars/.*

Sridhar, M. S. (1999). Skill requirements of LIS professionals in the new e-world. *Library science with a slant to documentation and, 36*(September), 141-149. Retrieved from *http://eprints.rclis.org/archive/00009637/*

Sridhar, M.S. (2004). Skill requirements of library professional in the Electronic Environment of Twenty first century. In Mahapatra, M. and Ramesh, D. B. *Information Technology application in libraries: A text book for beginners'* pp. 597-606

State Records of South Australia. (2009). Australian Standard AS ISO 15489 - Records Management. Retrieved from *www.archives.sa.gov.au.*

Trepath, S. M., Lal, C. and Kumar, K. (2002). Descriptive Question in Library and Information science. New Delhi, Ess-Ess Publication, p.161.

Verhulst, S. (2006). The regulation of digital content. In L. Lievrouw & S. Livingstone (Eds.), *The Handbook of New Media Updated Student Edition* (pp. 329-349). Sage.

Walsh, Virginia. (2010). The future of the library profession. *The Australian Library Journal.* 45(*4*). Retrieved from *http://www.alia.org.au/publishing/alj/archives/45.4/editorial.html*

Weaver, A C, Morrison, B B (2008). Social Networking. *Computer.* ACM. Retrieved from *http://ieeexplore.ieee.org/lpdocs/epic03/wrapper.htm?arnumber=4454412*

Young, O, Daley, E, Gualtieri, M, Lo, H, Ashour, M. (1995). The Mashup Opportunity. *Current,* (415), 168-173. IET. Retrieved from *http://www.forrester.com/Research/Document/Excerpt/0,7211,44213,00.html*

Epilogue

Library and Information Science profession is an ideal choice for those who are keen to serve society by providing "right information to right user at right time" and are willing to devote themselves for making the country information rich or push up towards knowledge based society. LIS professionals are honored to raise their helping hands for community members without consideration of age, sex, caste, religion, political background and economic condition, etc.

Presumptively the spirit of LIS professionals must be elevated if they can better review their shady past and analyze more completely and objectively the present problems. Library and information professional community is being affected by a range of ICT developments and so find its roles changing worldwide. A librarian with diverse talents and training, and who is flexible, will be able to meet the challenges of future library scene. The container of information is not only the print materials but this is the age we are living where a huge rate of information born in digital format. Technology alone cannot help bring about the required changes. Attitudes, practices, and policies need to change if libraries in India are to truly benefit themselves and their community of users by the application of new technologies. LIS professionals have been playing a versatile role beyond their traditional job. They have to gather adequate knowledge of computer and communication technologies, networks and networking, operating systems, Internet concepts, database management systems, along with adequate practical exposure to handle technological devices.

In mobilization of all kinds of information resources, librarians are expected to work as pathfinders by assisting all users with varied backgrounds and abilities through information supportive environment and multiple strategies.

There is a debate on the role of LIS professionals in near future. A group of people think that librarians will play a heightened role on activities such as, on time database searching, making them more visible. Rest suspect that the role of librarian will be deprofessionalised as users can get direct access to databases outside the library. Whatsoever, LIS professionals will play an indispensable role towards the knowledgebase society. Dependable professionalism certainly implies expertise, but it also means as awareness of developing needs of society what it expects. In a single sentence, the core functions of LIS professionals are unchanged whereas the mode of service is changing to cope with the paradigm shift.

Bibliography

Auer, Nicole J. & Ellen M. Krupar. (2001). Mouse click plagiarism: The role of technology plagiarism and the librarian's role in combating it. *Library Trend,* 49 (3) 415-32.

Baule, S. (1999). Information power: building partnerships for learning. Book Rep. 18(3): 42-43.

Carden, Mark. (2004). Library portals and enterprise portals: why libraries need to be at the centre of enterprise portal projects. *Information Services*, No.24. (pp.171-177)

Castelli D (2006). Digital libraries of the future – and the role of libraries. Library Hi Tech. 24(4): 496-503.

Chowdhury G G. (1994). Information retrieval system. Calcutta: IASLIC.

Chowdhury, G G. (2007). Organzing information: from the shelf to the web. London: Facet Publishing.

Cordeiro, Maria Ines. (2002). Web services: what they are and their importance for libraries. *VINE.* 32(4), pp.46-62.

Cox, Andrew. (2003). Choosing a library portal systems. *The Journal of Information and Knowledge Management Systems.* 33(1). (pp.37-41)

Fraze, James P. (2001). Charting a smooth course: for portal development. *Educause Quarterly*, No.3, (pp.42-48).

Ingwersen P. (1992). Information Retrieval Interaction. London:

Taylor Graham pp. 228.

Koneru, Indira. (2004). Library portal: effective information communication. ILA Golden Jubilee Conference, Knowledge Organisation in Digital *Environment in Libraries: Introspect and prospects*, 1-4 Dec, pp.327-335.

Lighthall, L (1990). Pivotal role of teacher-librarians. The Canadian School Executive,

Mangla, P. B. (1998). Library and information science education: trends and issues. In M. K. Jain (Ed.), *Fifty years of library and information services in India.* New Delhi: Shipra. pp.283-293.

Ranganathan, S.R. (1988). Five laws of library science Bangalore : Sarada Ranganathan Endowment for Library Science.

Sacchanand, Chutima. (1998, August). Distance Education in Library and Information Science in Asia and the Pacific Region. *Paper presented at 64th IFLA General Conference*, Amsterdam, Netherlands.

Svenonius, Elaine. (2000). The intellectual foundation of information organization. Cambridge: The MIT Press.

Index